modernism reborn

modernism reborn mid-century american houses

michael webb

principal photography by roger straus III

UNIVERSE

To Richard and Sandra Bergmann, keepers of the flame

First published in the United States of America in 2001
by UNIVERSE PUBLISHING
A Division of Rizzoli
International Publications, Inc.
300 Park Avenue South
New York, NY 10010

01 02 03 04 05 / 10 9 8 7 6 5 4 3 2 1

Editor: Terence Maikels
Book Design: Joseph Cho and Stefanie Lew, Binocular, New York

Manufactured in China

Library of Congress Card Number: 2001086838

Front cover photo: Pierre Koenig's Case Study house #21

Back cover photo: Cedric Gibbon's Dolores del Rio house

Frontispiece photos:
Previous spread: Pierre Koenig's Case Study house #21
Opposite: Richard Neutra's Kaufmann house

contents

introduction

Past speaks to present in this account of how a great vintage of residential architecture was created in the Depression and the two postwar decades, and how much of it has been saved by new and original owners for the delight of future generations. It offers a portrait of diversity, for mid-century modern encompasses radically different approaches to design, including fresh takes on the Arts and Crafts tradition, purist white stucco curves and cubes, lightweight post-and-beam structures, and houses inspired by machines. All reflected and fostered an adventurous way of living.

Owning and/or restoring a modern house makes a statement about one's individuality and taste. Lord Palumbo, the British financier, bought classics by Mies van der Rohe and Frank Lloyd Wright (along with a Le Corbusier in Paris) as compelling works of art. Tom Ford of Gucci expressed his love of simplicity by asking Los Angeles specialists Marmol and Radziner to recreate a plain Richard Neutra villa. Martha Stewart brought in British minimalist John Pawson to enhance her Gordon Bunshaft in East Hampton. But, for every millionaire or celebrity commissioning architects to upgrade a landmark, many more owners are investing sweat equity in houses that afford them the same quiet satisfaction.

This book is about that effort and those rewards. A lucky few have the gift of spotting an old master painting under layers of yellowing varnish, or the inherent beauty of a classic car that has turned to rust. With a run-down house, the challenge is greater, even when you know who designed it. You have to decide how authentic a restoration you want, how long you can take (while lodging elsewhere or living on a construction site), and how much you can afford to spend. As with a painting, you can go too far and destroy the uniqueness that drew you in the first place; however, architecture is more elastic than art, and allows you to add, remodel, and redecorate in the spirit of the original. You can even juxtapose radically different structures and furnishings, provided you respect the character and scale of what was there before.

Mid-century modern houses were often commissioned by maverick clients, who overrode the opposition of stick-in-the-mud neighbors and officials to create something tailored to their needs and desires. Often they shared their architects' vision of creating a brave new world of rational plans and unornamented planes, lightweight construction and free-flowing volumes, transparency and openness. However, those concepts were first developed, not for middle-class villas, but to improve the lives of the masses. In Holland, Germany, Switzerland, and Scandinavia, municipalities, industrial corporations, and nonprofit organizations embraced modernism as the logical way of upgrading cities and workplaces and creating new communities.

In Europe, the catalyst was World War I—a bloodbath so brutal and irrational that it destroyed the credibility of the old order, brought political and economic chaos, and gave birth to the best and worst of the modern age. The Russian Revolution and countless manifestos inspired progressive thinkers to act. Model housing, schools, sanatoria, and public buildings went up all over northern Europe and even in Mussolini's Italy. Modernism became part of the everyday landscape, briefly subduing conservative resistance to change and the average person's dislike of the unfamiliar. The Bauhaus was fiercely unpopular among provincial Germans, but it made a lasting impact on that country and, eventually, the world.

Modernism enjoyed an early flowering in southern California. A benign climate fostered informality and outdoor living, allowing flat roofs, sheer white stucco walls, and expansive windows—a design vocabulary that proved more appropriate there than in northern Europe. R.M. Schindler and Richard Neutra came to America from Vienna to work for Frank Lloyd Wright and then stayed on to practice in Los Angeles. The houses each created for Dr. Philip Lovell still have the power to astonish. However, their efforts, like the West Coast experiments of Wright and Irving Gill, went almost unnoticed in the rest of the country, which was still in thrall to picturesque eclecticism and had almost no appreciation for the avant-garde.

Through the 1920s, the majority of Americans were too busy making money or pursuing pleasure to share in the anguished intellectual debates of Europe. The economic boom reinforced native complacency and philistinism, foreigners and their ideas were widely mistrusted, and even moderate socialism was regarded as a dangerous disease. In architecture schools, the nineteenth-century Beaux Arts curriculum was unchallenged. Residential architecture was shaped by developers and the market, not paternalistic authorities and iconoclastic reformers—as it is still today. However, the early years of the Depression eroded public confidence in the establishment, as World War I had done in Europe. The trauma of tottering banks and mass unemployment, which destroyed democracies and halted many experiments abroad, spread fresh thinking in the United States.

Hollywood briefly flirted with streamline moderne, hiring out-of-work architects to design sleek penthouses and nightclubs as backdrops for Greta Garbo in bias-cut satin or Fred Astaire in white tie and tails. For a few years, the movies promoted modernism as shorthand for all that was smart and sophisticated, but producers soon realized they were getting far ahead of their audience, in terms of both decor and morality. From 1933 on, modernity reverted to its traditional role as the hallmark of villains and femmes fatales; loyal

10 wives and mothers aspired to Colonial and chintz armchairs. As historian Esther McCoy later observed, "modern houses were a badge of intellectual emancipation; the less venturesome and more domestic women preferred a Cape Cod or a ranch house."

In 1932, at the depth of the Depression, Philip Johnson and Henry Russell Hitchcock curated the landmark *Modern Architecture: International Exhibition* at the newly founded Museum of Modern Art in New York and authored a book, *The International Style: Architecture Since 1922*. The exhibition was shown around the country, in museums and department stores, and helped introduce the general public to modernism. The curators were aesthetes, not radicals; they celebrated the new European work (and a few American examples) as pure form, stripped of its social and political agendas for domestic consumption.

How different was the response of Count Harry Kessler, a progressive German aristocrat and keen observer of the contemporary scene. In a 1932 entry in his diary (recently published as *Berlin in Lights*), he recounts driving the writer André Gide around a new housing estate in Berlin and telling him: "To look on this architecture simply as architecture, art for art's sake so to speak, is to miss its point. It has to be understood as a new way of living, a new assessment of what life is for and how it should be lived." Earlier, he had told another French visitor, the artist Aristide Maillol, that this phenomenon was the expression of vitality and the youthful cult of nudity and sports.

Conservative Americans were shocked by nudity in buildings as in people, but they favored anything that would restore the economy. Capitalism vied with communism, promising a brave new world through technology during the Depression as it did at the height of the Cold War. Big corporations sponsored visionary scenarios at the Chicago Century of Progress Exhibition in 1933–34 and the New York World's Fair of 1939–40. Huge crowds shuffled through Houses of the Future at these popular extravaganzas and assuaged their longings by purchasing streamlined toasters. As the Depression eased in the late 1930s, modernism began to gain momentum in American residential architecture. Land and construction costs were so low, especially in southern California, that even a schoolteacher or a movie studio musician could afford to build a one-of-a-kind house, its tiny rooms augmented by an expansive garden and a view.

World War II halted most construction, while building high expectations for the peace. Victory brought a sense of exhilaration, for it was seen as a triumph of American improvisation and know-how. Progressive architects were moved by social need and the deprivation of the Depression and war. Many returned from combat with a burning desire to create a better world. They responded enthusiastically to the challenge of exploiting new materials and techniques, designing artifacts and houses that could be mass-produced in the factories that had churned out bombers and tanks.

Los Angeles was one center of activity. Gregory Ain designed several low-budget planned communities, working with enlightened individuals and associations, much as European progressives had. John Entenza, the idealistic editor of *Arts + Architecture* magazine, commissioned 36 Case Study House designs from Pierre Koenig, Craig Ellwood, Rafael Soriano, Charles and Ray Eames, and other inventive talents of southern California. Elegance and practicality were combined in these prototypes for a fresh lifestyle. They featured expansive glazing and an easy flow of space from open living areas and kitchens to a yard that was treated as an outdoor room. Most were designed for young families without servants, and their innovations gradually trickled down to the mass market. (They also inspired young architects as far afield as Australia and New Zealand.)

To the north, builder Joseph Eichler created tracts of inexpensive modern houses in the San Francisco Bay Area. In Sarasota, Florida, Paul Rudolph designed light, airy residences that adapted well to the subtropical climate. However, the most surprising enclave of innovation in the 1950s was New Canaan, Connecticut: a conservative Colonial town of 80,000 where Harvard graduates Eliot Noyes, Philip Johnson, and John Johansen settled with their mentor, Marcel Breuer. There they socialized and built, luring kindred spirits and creating a legacy that is now fought over by preservationists and developers. Happily, there is a growing appreciation of the legacy.

In the 1950s, most progressive architects took modernism for granted—it was the way you built, a basic syntax—and they enjoyed a strong sense of collegiality. But, their dreams of rational design and factory production had been usurped by home-builders and unions that saw no point in changing profitable and moderately efficient methods of construction. Bank loan officers were as timidly conservative as ever, and the vast majority of Americans, once they had a choice, opted for an ornamental overlay on their stucco boxes. Modernism remained a minority taste, but there was a steady demand that kept its practitioners productive. "The group was more important than the individual—it was cool to be anonymous," Koenig recalls. "Designers were trying to create better, cheaper ways of living: it was the second half of the century versus the first—an era of optimism that was destroyed by the turbulence and inflation of the late 'sixties."

By the mid 1960s, architects had seen and responded to Le Corbusier's chapel at Ronchamp and other sculptural buildings. They had broken out of the box and the old orthodoxy seemed dead. Then

12 modernism itself came under attack—from Robert Venturi, arguing for complexity and contradiction in architecture; Peter Blake, deploring shoddy, inhumane construction; and Jane Jacobs, excoriating massive urban renewal. As America grew disenchanted with the idea of progress and swung to the right, trend-spotter Tom Wolfe cleverly repackaged xenophobia and philistinism in his polemic *From Bauhaus to Our House*. Others piled into the fray, and homeowners who wanted to foster the illusion of an "olde towne" in featureless suburbs started mandating pitched roofs and picket fences.

An architecture that had been introduced to America as a style and had never put down deep roots was easily displaced by other fashions. It never went away, but it did go out of favor. A few classic modern houses were lovingly preserved by their original owners, but many more suffered neglect and abuse. The huge growth of wealth in the 1980s and 1990s had a devastating impact. "Modest modernists edged out by McMansions," read a recent headline in the *Vancouver Courier*, and the same could be said for communities across the United States. Realtors urged buyers to tear down houses that appeared to have outlived their usefulness or to be too small for their sites, and indulge in the American cult of gigantism and conspicuous consumption. Builders eagerly responded to the call, loading their special offerings with such essential amenities as marble tubs with gold faucets, crystal chandeliers, and gyms that would easily accommodate an Olympic team.

In reaction to this second Gilded Age, discerning nonconformists have embraced the frugal or daring experiments of fifty years ago. The concept of mid-century modern began with 1950s furnishings—typically boomerang tables, Eames chairs, and George Nelson clocks—and mutated into an appreciation for the architecture of the era immediately before and after World War II. Interest has grown as that time recedes into history, becoming a product of the last century. Neglected gems by Neutra, Breuer, Lautner, Harris, and Rudolph are being snapped up, and the search has widened to include works by architects who never achieved fame or were forgotten.

Houses that were once viewed as brash and shocking, and may have been conceived as subversive statements, appear to a new generation as period artifacts, enhanced by the patina of age. I live in one of a group of apartments near UCLA that Neutra designed in 1937 as income property. He had a hard time leasing them, for unadorned white cubes stacked on a bare hillside scared off prospective tenants, and some went away muttering "moon architecture!" A fellow Austrian, the Academy Award–winning actress Luise Rainer, moved in and wrote to Neutra that she had always been afraid of modern houses, thinking them cold and unwelcoming. "How different it is," she exclaimed, "the moment you live inside! The clearness, the long lines of windows which allow the light to come in and the eye to rove out, all this gives you a strange feeling of happiness and freedom." The Eameses lived here through the 1940s, and their apartment inspired the first design for their house.

The growing popularity of mid-century modern has a more solid foundation than the cycle of fashion and a reaction against excess. The best of these houses have a timeless beauty, harmonious proportions, clean lines, openness, and abundant natural light. They represent a triumph of honesty over pretense, and their simplicity inspires nostalgia for what is now perceived to be a more innocent era. (How the boomers do love their misty-eyed recollections of childhood!)

Even the spareness can be an attraction. Architects were working hard to eliminate excess pounds from their work long before the rest of humanity became obsessed with hard bodies. Today, these houses seem to have taken their turn at the gym and provide flattering frames for their well-toned owners. Living within constraints with a minimum of clutter and doing without the walk-in closets, luxury spas, and great rooms that your neighbors find indispensable brings a sense of virtue. In fact, these open-plan houses correspond more closely to the casual, unstructured lifestyle of today's young couples—dressing down, working from laptops in bed or on a sofa, and eating on the run—than they did to patterns of living a half century ago.

Allyn Morris, who designed a bold house for himself that is now cherished by a youthful producer, observed: "If a house isn't happy, it's a failure. You have to be young at heart, which is why young people are buying modern houses and putting them back to what they were."

Too few people share this passion, and too many remarkable modern houses are still being trashed. Perhaps the title of this book should be: "Don't tear it down!" Good architecture has always been a scarce resource, and the best modern buildings deserve as much care and respect as those from earlier eras. Preservationists are often swayed by sentiment and fight for picturesque fragments while ignoring extraordinary work of the past 50 years. Only a limited amount of construction can—or should—be saved. Merit, not age, should be the yardstick, and posterity will judge us harshly if we neglect this principle.

brave new world

Few could afford to build during the Great Depression, but everyone dreamed of a brighter future, and a few landmark houses expressed that spirit of hope. Architects and designers played inventive variations on the rigorous geometry and open plans of International Modern, softening the lines, combining traditional building materials with steel and white stucco, and introducing decorative elements without compromising the purity of the whole.

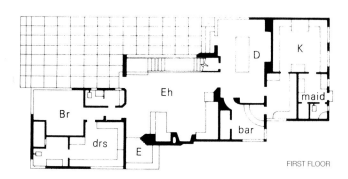

FIRST FLOOR

dolores del rio house

santa monica, california
cedric gibbons &
douglas honnold
1930
restored 1981 –

In its years of greatness, from the mid 1920s through the mid 1950s, Metro-Goldwyn-Mayer was the embodiment of Hollywood glamour and style. Everything that appeared behind the actors required the approval of Cedric Gibbons, the studio's supervising art director. He personally created one enduring set—a love nest for himself and his new wife, the Mexican star Dolores del Rio. Though the 5,000-square-foot house was partly designed by Douglas

Honnold, an architect who worked at M-G-M and later began a residential practice, the concept is pure Gibbons. It embodies his impeccable taste (always a dark blue suit and a gleaming white Duesenberg), his enthusiasm for modernity, and his mastery of scenic effects. Happily, the house has been restored to pristine condition by the progressive developer Ira Yellin and his social activist wife, Adele, who have lived here since 1981.

The street façade is as bare as the wall of a sound stage, focusing attention on the gray metal door with its asymmetrical frame of angled setbacks. You pass through into a light-filled reception room, looking out through horizontally framed

windows to a palm-shaded terrace, which steps down to a pool. Light gleams off polished black linoleum, stepped white walls and ceilings, and the nickel-plated steel stair balustrade. The staircase has shallow white terrazzo treads, is silhouetted against the far wall, and was made for eye-catching entrances: the star descends from heaven to greet her guests, then leads them back up to the 45-by-25-foot living room with its step-vaulted ceiling. Architecture critic Paul Goldberger aptly describes the interior as "an essay in the composition of setbacks…a place to be moved through rather than to be seen in repose…designed for nighttime entertaining."

Gibbons delighted his bride with concealed lighting, the illusion of a full moon on a white wall, and a summer shower that pattered on the copper roof whenever a sprinkler system was activated. However, there is much more to the house than ingenious effects and luxurious details. In contrast to the shallow deception of a movie set, which is habitable only on screen, and the geometric austerity of contemporary European modernism, this is a house that rewards the senses as well as the intellect. Spaces are layered and varied, and wall mirrors add another dimension to each room. The house is rectalinear, except for a curved passage that leads to a breakfast room with a shallow cove-lit dome, and yet the

Opposite Horizontal steel-framed windows look out over a palm-shaded terrace and steps leading down to the pool.

19

overall effect is sensual, not hard-edged. Stepped moldings, cubistic fireplaces, and built-in banquettes all act as scaling devices to balance the sweep of the public areas, while cove lighting and backlit stair treads enhance the magic at night. Karen Carsello helped the owners select leather club chairs and flared aluminum torchères that subtly reinforce the streamlined spirit of the interior.

Private rooms, even the subdued master bedroom, are intimately scaled. The master bathrooms have retained their original Vitrolite panels, wrap-around mirrors, black marble basins, and floor controls for the faucets. Michael Beckson turned a guest bedroom into a private office, and Rogerio Carvalherio has customized a Bulthaup kitchen, adding white tiles and zebrawood to perpetuate the spirit of the old.

The exterior required more radical attention. Brenda Levin designed a new street gate of stainless steel and oxidized copper to replace the crumbling original. The cubic tennis pavilion, which resembles a proscenium arch from the court, retained its stair balustrade of copper hoops, but the new owners had to replace with vinyl the copper-framed linoleum panels on the walls and step-vaulted ceiling, which had been painted pink, and remove Astroturf from the concrete floor. The terrace was re-paved, and palms and other ex-otics replaced ailing pines. Lights! Camera! Action! This house is again ready for its close-up.

Opposite The upstairs living room evokes a set from a glamorous M-G-M star-vehicle of the 1930s.

Above A white terrazzo staircase with a nickel-plated steel balustrade leads up from the reception area.

Top Mirrors and a polished black floor make the living room seem even larger than it is.

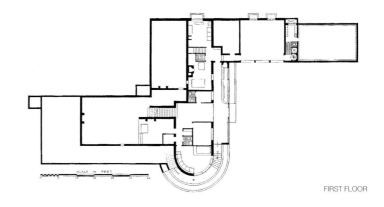

mandel house

bedford hills, new york
edward durell stone
1933–34
restored 1992–

Rarely has a house enjoyed a more auspicious debut. For the prestigious magazine *Architectural Forum*, it resembled "a giant airplane [that] seems to partake of the openness of the landscape and sky." *Fortune* headlined it "The House that Works" and, with wildly misplaced optimism, cited it as evidence of America's love affair with the machine, the first wave of a modernist tide that would sweep away "the false, faked, footling inconveniences erected

in the 'twenties." Stone would end his career doing "harem-classical" buildings, as architecture critic Ada Louise Huxtable called them, but this house demonstrated his passing infatuation with modernism, which he had witnessed firsthand in Europe, and led to other prestigious commissions, including the design, with Richard Goodwin, of the Museum of Modern Art in New York.

The youthful architect met his client while working with designer Donald Deskey on the interiors of Radio City Music Hall. Richard Mandel, heir to a department store fortune, was an ardent modernist who had become Deskey's partner and invited him to create the interiors and furniture for the house. The

Mandels spent $60,000—a high price at that time—and had twenty years to enjoy the house. It survived neglect and harsh winters in surprisingly good condition, with most of its furnishings still in place—including the Deskey piano, which George Gershwin may have played.

Eric Brill, a former oil trader, and his wife, Nanette, were searching for vintage modern, saw this house in a book on the 1930s, and tracked it down through a local historian. It took them four years to buy it from the Japanese family that lived there, and it will take them much

Above A dining table by Donald Deskey and chairs by Gilbert Rohde seem to float within this glass bay.

Opposite From the entry to the right, the house appears as a masterly interplay of geometric forms.

longer, with the enthusiastic support of their three children, to restore it to its original condition, working from period photographs and a stack of blueprints.

Already, the house looks pristine as you approach it up the sloping drive. It suggests a beached liner more than an airplane, with its three stacked decks extending away from a curved bay that could be the ship's bridge; its taut white skin alternates with the delicate green glazing bars of the ribbon windows. From the outside, it is a poster child for International Modern, but Stone absorbed only the look—not the substance—of the movement. The east side offers a wonderful interplay of forms, but the glass entry has no canopy and seems almost an afterthought, as though the architect had been reluctant to open his beautiful package.

The impact of the interior owes more to Deskey's spare, metal-framed chairs and tables—along with atmospheric, indirect lighting—than to the flow of space. The plan is almost old-fashioned. The kitchen and the servants' rooms (plus a squash court) are located to one side of a spinal wall; living areas and family bedrooms are on the other side of the divide. In a servantless age, the 10,500 square feet feel very stretched out.

You enter between a solarium with a cactus growing in a planter beneath the window, and a sophisticated bar with an illuminated counter top, a turquoise

Opposite The house is entered through a solarium with a planter of cactus; a horseshoe bar opens off to one side.

Above A beached liner with decks extending away from a curved bridge: the epitome of streamline moderne

leather banquette that the Brills found in storage, and a re-creation of the original mural on the pleasures of drinking. Stairs with elegant aluminum rails lead up to the spacious second-floor living room, newly enhanced with a room-height mirror around the fireplace at the far end, and a wood-paneled library in one corner. The most dramatic space is the dining room, with its black terrazzo floor, tall windows flanked by glass blocks, and the backlit bakelite-topped Deskey table and Gilbert Rohde chairs. Most of the other rooms are unremarkable, but the excitement returns when you step out onto one of the five raised terraces for a look at the sweeping views and the dynamic massing of the house.

The flat roof has been resur-faced, and a gaping hole and 70 broken windows have been repaired. (The previous owners complained of high heating bills!) Each spring, the Brills have tackled another area of water-damaged plaster and peeling paint. They have acquired a painted bedroom set, pool table, and other furniture by Deskey and his contemporaries to flesh out the original pieces, adding posters from the Russian Revo-lution and a Harley-Davidson Electra Glide as grace notes. They are presently planning to refurbish the worn cork floor tiles and replace damaged glass blocks.

Opposite Ribbon windows wrap around the spacious living room with its original furniture and cork-tile floor.

Above A guest bedroom with painted wood furniture by Donald Deskey

Top A handsomely railed staircase links the three levels of the house.

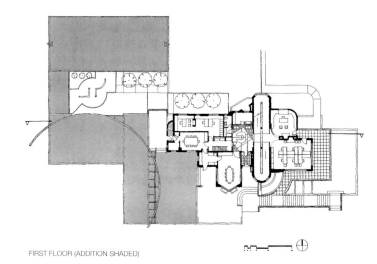

FIRST FLOOR (ADDITION SHADED)

butler house

des moines, iowa
george kraetsch
1934–36
restored and extended by
douglas wells of wells
woodburn o'neill, 1988–89

"Concentrate for a year or two on planning a house and, no matter whether it is large or small, you will spend the rest of your life enjoying it," declared Earl Butler after realizing his dream of a residence so comfortable he wouldn't want to travel any more. As a young man he had picked the eleven-acre hilltop site outside the city. He then spent half a lifetime as a nomad, managing investments and real estate, before buying the land and beginning his

collaboration with George Kraetsch, a local architect and friend, on this 13,000-square-foot residence. Every aspect of construction was worked out on paper before the design began. The steel-frame structure would resist tornadoes, and the dense concrete would be poured into plywood forms to achieve a smooth maintenance-free finish. Butler consulted the blueprints as he went through his daily routine, imagining how he would use the spaces they detailed. He invited his wife's friends to test his lighting set-ups and visited showrooms in order to try out tubs for size, jumping in while fully dressed.

A hands-on Midwesterner, uninterested in theory or fashion, Butler was concerned only that

everything in the house be the best of its kind and fully tested—from the electric eye that opened the garage doors to the intercom and air conditioning. "Surplus materials for decorative purposes are totally lacking," he later observed, "as I believe that simplicity and good design are much more restful and inherently beautiful in a home." He probably missed MoMA's Modern Architecture exhibition, and his wife expressed her preference for a Colonial, but he convinced himself and her that modern was the way to go—just as *Fortune* had predicted.

Kraetsch may have seen designer Norman Bel Geddes's 1932 book *Horizons*, with its sketches of futuristic ships and planes, and a soberly practical

"House of the Future." The Butler house, however, is an original—especially in the brilliantly composed south front, where the entrance is flanked by rounded and angled two-story bays with setback wings and is unified by a band of incised lines that serves as a stylized cornice. Rising from the flat roof is a library with a round-cornered canopy and outdoor hearth that is almost a miniature of the house. A side window has an eyelid canopy, but the rest of the house is crisp and cubistic, set off by curved steps and flat section aluminum rails. Like Le Corbusier's Villa Savoye, it seems to float on an expansive lawn—an enticing vision of a brave new world.

The 28 rooms open off a wide ramp to east and west,

Opposite An enticing vision of a brave new world of concrete and glass: the south façade

and their floors are staggered to minimize the incline. The ramp serves seven levels, flattening out at each landing, making it easy to entertain throughout the house, whether for muddy hunters cooking their game in the basement or a summer party on the roof. Much of the original hardware is still in place—from the rolldown mesh screens on the thermopane windows to the built-in speakers. There is an extraordinary variety of light fittings, functional and decorative, which include a ceiling box in the dining room with red, blue, and yellow tubes, each separately dimmed, behind molded glass. Bel Geddes was an innovative theater designer and may have inspired Kraetsch; General Electric used

the house as a demonstration project.

Advertising executive Jack Kraigie bought the house in 1988, after it had served two decades as a bible college. He commissioned Douglas Wells to restore the major spaces (including Butler's library-study with its curved sliding door and oak cabinets), replace worn windows, and repaint the house white, inside and out. To accomodate a staff of 35, Wells remodeled peripheral rooms and embedded a new office in the hillside. A second office was later constructed to the rear of the house. Though these additions and the office setups within the house are far from ideal, they have ensured the survival of a glorious period piece that is still up-to-date. Thanks to Kraigie, a future owner would find it easy to undo all the changes, upgrade the furnishings, and restore the house to its original role as a showcase of progressive living.

29

Opposite A broad ramp leads up through the house to provide easy access for guests.

Above A hearth is built into the side of the rooftop library for outdoor entertaining.

Top The ramp is flattened at each of the seven staggered levels to either side.

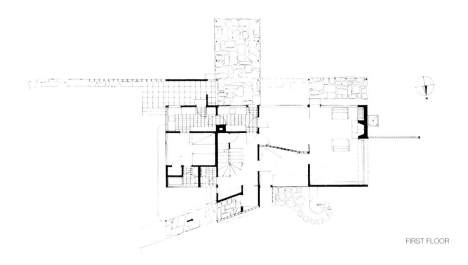

gropius house

lincoln, massachusetts
walter gropius
1937 – 38
restored 1984 – 85, 1998 –
2001

A short walk from Walden Pond is a house that was as revolutionary in its day as were the shots heard around the world in nearby Concord. Walter Gropius was the visionary who founded the Bauhaus in 1919 and brought its message to the United States in 1937. His first American building was this 2,300-square-foot home, which he built for his family in the village of Lincoln, a half-hour drive from his new job as a professor at the Harvard Graduate School of Design. A crisp white presence on a grassy hillside, the house is a showcase of modernist principles infused with the practicality of the Colonial vernacular. The plain geometry, straight roofline, and ribbon windows recall the houses that Gropius and Marcel Breuer had designed for the Bauhaus masters in Dessau twelve years before. The taut skin of vertical clapboards rising from a fieldstone base, the screen porch and the fences that extend from either side, and the central stair hall with rooms opening off on two levels are features that the architect admired in New England farmhouses.

Luck played a role in the realization of the house. A German professor convinced a hostile Joseph Goebbels that the Nazis could gain a propaganda advantage by allowing Gropius to retrieve the contents of his Berlin apartment, and this collection of Bauhaus furnishings needed an appropriate setting. Gropius, his wife, Ise, and their adopted daughter, Ati, rented a cottage and loved the novel experience of living close to the land, but were unable to secure a mortgage for an unconventional design. Hearing that this new immigrant was being prevented from showing what he could do, a philanthropic landowner, Mrs. James Storrow, offered building plots to Gropius and Breuer, loaned them money, and allowed them to rent their homes until they could repay her—despite the fact that she, an elderly woman, was wedded to tradition. Ise Gropius returned the favor by donating her house to the Society for the Preservation of New England Antiquities (SPNEA), which assumed responsibility after her death in 1983 and undertook a major restoration before opening it to the public.

For Peter Gittleman, the architect who supervised the SPNEA effort, there was a double challenge: to restore materials and fixtures that were no longer in production, and to capture the spirit of the house as it was at a specific moment in time, working from period photographs and the memories of Ati Gropius Johansen. The SPNEA selected 1967 as their base date, because little had

Opposite A cantilevered entrance canopy and exterior stair animate the plain north façade.

survived from the first three decades. The owners had had no sentimental attachment to the shabby or outdated; when an old piece broke it was trashed and replaced with a new item from Knoll or Design Research. For the SPNEA, authenticity and the patina of age are priorities; for Gropius's daughter, the right look is more important than the historically correct, and she continues to argue her case with the passion of an insider.

This was a novel experience for an institution whose other properties are centuries old. Like Gropius, its members became pioneers, tracing sources for plastics that had dried out, veneers that had swollen from creeping damp, and laminates that had begun to flake. They matched original paint colors, including the Bauhaus pink that artist Lyonel Feininger had put on the wall of the second-floor deck, and stripped and re-painted the exterior walls when they discovered that mildew retardant, added by Gropius, had caused repeated peeling. A craftsman replaced single-glazed metal windows that are out of production, but no satisfactory substitute has been found for broken glass blocks in the wall that screens the entry, since Corning sold the molds in South America. Within, the acoustic plaster of walls and ceilings has been sponged clean, and new cork floor tiles installed—though these are thinner than the originals and have quickly bleached.

Opposite A base of local stone anchors the crisp white box, and a fence extends it into the landscape.

Top Play of light and shadow on the roof terrace. Lyonel Feininger contributed the Bauhaus pink wall.

Above The geometry of the house is enlivened by personal touches like this hand-welded steel stair rail.

Meticulous restoration and Ati's breezy irreverence have combined to preserve a sense of vitality that is often lacking in house museums. Visitors can enjoy the property on two levels at once: as a daring experiment, crammed with fresh ideas and novel artifacts, and as an enduring part of the New England heritage. Early settlers adapted European models to the local climate and building materials; Gropius did the same, rooting modernism in this stony soil, and impressing skeptical neighbors by riding out the great hurricane of 1938. Gittleman describes this as the home of an intellectual, not a sensualist—all clean lines and functional furnishings—but it is full of personal touches, from the sinuous hand-welded steel stair rail to the glass wall between bedroom and dressing area that allowed the owners to sleep with open windows while conserving heat in the rest of the house. Gropius deplored Americans who built Tudor houses and returned from work in skyscrapers to squeeze into a fairy-tale world that had nothing to do with the way they lived. In this frugal, compact, energy-efficient house he showed them a better way—as Thoreau had for his contemporaries almost a century before.

Tours are offered from 11am–4pm on weekends, year-round, and on Wednesdays–Fridays, June 1–October 15. Information: (781) 259-8098; http://www.spnea.org.

Opposite Gropius furnished the living room with Bauhaus pieces from his Berlin apartment, a few of which still survive.

Above The tightly compressed staircase links the entry hall to the bedrooms.

Top A porch with detachable mesh screens projects from the south façade and was used for summer dining.

fusing craft and innovation

Modernism emerged from the late nineteenth-century Arts and Crafts movement, which sought to revive hand-craftsmanship and the use of natural materials while eliminating decorative excess. Successive generations of forward-looking architects have found inspiration in these principles and have built upon them in their own work, achieving a satisfying combination of tactility and invention.

saarinen house

bloomfield hills, michigan
eliel saarinen
1928–30
restored by gregory wittkopp,
1988–94

Like his compatriot Alvar Aalto, Eliel Saarinen combined traditional forms and craftsmanship with progressive ideas to create an alternate version of modernism—both in his native Finland and his adopted America. Acclaimed by his peers for his second-place entry in the 1922 competition for the Chicago Tribune Tower, he moved to the Midwest the following year, and designed much of the Cranbrook Educational Community. As first president of the Cranbrook Academy of Art (1932–46), he made it an American version of the Bauhaus, nurturing the careers of his son, Eero; Charles and Ray Eames; and Harry Bertoia, among many others.

The house-studio he built on the campus for himself and his wife, Loja, is a fascinating hybrid. The Arts and Crafts exterior of brick, tile, and leaded lights tells nothing about the interior, which fuses neo-classicism with decorative modernism. It looks back to Hvittrask, the house on a Finnish lake that Saarinen designed with two young contemporaries as an early expression of Romantic Nationalism, and forward to the open light-filled volumes, bare surfaces, and geometric patterns of functionalism. The velvet portieres that dramatize the entrances to the principal rooms can be seen either as an echo of nineteenth-century gentility or as a device to soften sharp edges—as Mies did in his Barcelona Pavilion. The house is equally hospitable to Eero's tubular metal chairs in the studio and his streamlined bedroom furniture.

Five presidents of the Cranbrook Academy lived in the house, and Saarinen's successors modernized it to suit their own needs and reflect contemporary fashion. Wall coverings were removed, acoustic tiles installed, and subtle tones were overpainted white. Rugs and the fabrics that were woven on campus to Loja's designs wore out, and the oak block floors were carpeted, but the house remained structurally sound—for it had been built, at great expense, to institutional standards. Roy Slade, who became president in 1977, began to refurbish the interior. After ten years of discovering its beauty, he put Gregory Wittkopp, an architect and the curator of collections, in charge of a full-scale restoration. This accelerated in 1990, when Slade moved into the lesser house Saarinen designed next door, allowing his own to become a house museum.

The Saarinens' sensibilities enriched and refined the house for several years after its completion. Wittkopp decided to use the late 1930s as his benchmark for restoration, working from about 25 photos that

Above The Arts and Crafts exterior with its brick, tile, and leaded lights, gives no hint of the interiors.

Opposite The living room from the entry hall, with the studio opening off to the left

40

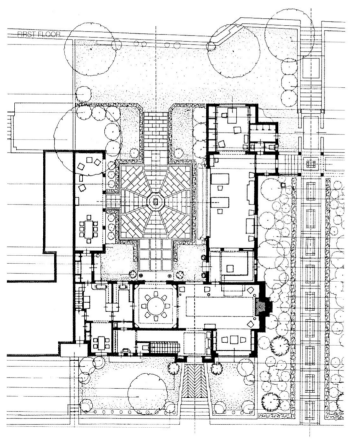

FIRST FLOOR

documented the interiors and striving for authenticity of materials and finishes. On the living room walls, he replaced the jute cloth that Eliel Saarinen had substituted for a short-lived experimental mix of jute and rayon, dying the bleached fabric to conform to the natural tone of the original. Paint analysis indicated that other walls were originally a uniform pale gray, but the photos contradicted this. Wittkopp realized this first coat must have been done in a rush to get the house ready for the owners, who were returning from a summer in Finland. The tests were repeated and showed that the second coats were subtly varied in tone.

Detective work played an important role in the restoration. The rift-cut straight-grain fir veneers that were used in the paneling of the dining room are no longer available, but something similar was found in storage in Grand Rapids. Traces of lime at the base of the wall indicated that the wood had been bleached before it was beeswaxed. The soft glow of the fir is again a foil to the Chinese red of the side niches, the regilded dome, and the Art Deco table and chairs that Saarinen designed for this room. Analysis revealed that the maple shelves in the book room had been quickly rubbed with black and white, cleaned off, and protected with demar varnish, which breathes and remains clear. As an amateur painter, Saarinen must have used it on

Above The barrel-vaulted studio, as seen from Eliel Saarinen's office, with chairs designed by his son, Eero

his canvases, and it gives a pleasing matte finish; however, moisture causes it to cloud, and so the window ledges are protected with polyurethane varnish, which is shinier but resists condensation. Rugs and fabrics were rewoven to the original designs and missing pieces of furniture were reproduced, though most of the key pieces had survived.

Saarinen's desk occupies one of the raised alcoves at the ends of the long, barrel-vaulted studio, which doubled as a reception area. The owners' personal tastes are, however, best revealed in the private rooms upstairs. The master bathroom, with its expanses of plain tile and Vitrolite and its functional ceiling lights, complements the bedroom—which was furnished

softly by Loja and severely by Eero. Thanks to Wittkopp and his expert helpers on and off campus, the house is pristine, yet has a subtle patina befitting its age and the artistry that shaped it.

Tours are offered at 1:30pm Tuesdays–Fridays, and at 1:30 and 3pm on weekends, May–October. Twilight tours are offered at 7:30pm on Fridays, June–August. Information: (248) 645-3361; http://www.cranbrook.edu.

Left Velvet portieres separate the dining room with its gilded dome and wall niches from the living room.

Above Functional lighting and plain tile gives a crisp modern character to the master bathroom.

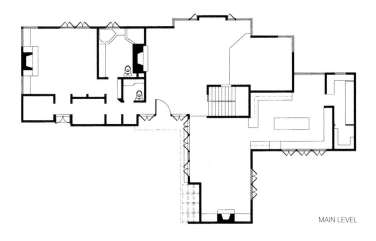

MAIN LEVEL

evans house

brentwood, california
lloyd wright
1936–37, 1941
restored by harold zellman
1993–95

Through his six decades of practice, Frank Lloyd Wright Jr.—who was always known as Lloyd—struggled to emerge from the shadow of his famous father. In the early 1920s in Los Angeles their careers intertwined, as both explored the expressive potential of knit concrete blocks, and the son rose to eminence as the master suffered an eclipse. This reversal of fortune was short-lived, for Lloyd Wright never again matched the power and vision of his father, and some of his subsequent houses are little more than eccentric curiosities.

One of the best of his residences was commissioned by Warwick Evans, a studio musician, and his wife, Elizabeth. Architect and clients all played the cello, and the 3,200-square-foot house evokes a romantic concerto in its dramatic structure, with long lyrical passages, sudden surprises, and graceful ornament. As with so much of Wright's work, it displays a combination of traditional and progressive themes. Impeccably crafted paneling and angled vaults over the principal rooms evoke a Greene and Greene bungalow, while the easy flow of space through the interior and out the steel-framed windows generates a sense of openness and light that is quintessentially modern. From below, the house reveals only straight lines; the pitched roofs come into view as you ascend the slope. Narrow stairs lead up from the entry to the sitting room, bar, and dining room. Each room gains space from its neighbor, its vault, and from expansive windows. Extending from the main living area are a low-ceilinged study and skylit kitchen; opposite is the master suite, which is bathed in light from three sides. A carport and the children's bedrooms are unobtrusively tucked beneath the main floor.

"The Evans house had gone through six owners, had been significantly changed, and was in terrible disrepair when I found it," says Michael Rabkin, a cosmetic surgeon who bought the property with his wife, Ginger, in 1989. "But it had a presence I liked, so I secured the plans to discover what had been there originally and started tearing the house apart, layer by layer."

It took architect Harold Zellman two years to remove unsightly additions, refurbish the original fabric (most of which remained intact), and replace what was missing. The goals were to restore the character and look of the house as closely as possible to what they had been in the late 1930s, bring the structure up to code, upgrade the kitchen and bathrooms, and install new services. The exterior was sandblasted down to the original integrally

Opposite In the second floor living areas, vaulted ceilings complement the steel-framed windows to achieve a fusion of modern and moderne.

44 colored green-and-cream stucco. Within, the elegant stair railing had buckled as the house settled. It was necessary to jack up the structure in order to remove and restore the wrought iron, after which ten layers of paint were stripped and the ball ornaments regilded. Cypress paneling and a copper chimney hood were revealed behind sheetrock; the hardwood floor was unearthed from beneath several coats of white paint.

As did Adolf Loos, Wright used rich natural materials in place of applied ornament. Every surface invites a caress. The matched grain in the cypress veneer plays off the onyx, patinaed copper, and layered sandstone of the various fireplaces. Sunlight filters in through wood venetian blinds, spilling across the polished wood floor. At night, soft cove lighting in the vaults is supplemented by downlights and the glow of lamps by Raymond Loewy, Walter von Nessen, and other notable designers of the 1930s. The effect is warm and romantic, with a dash of Raymond Chandler and *Chinatown*.

"We got hooked on modernism," says Rabkin, "and began collecting American pieces as we restored the house." He discovered from photographs that the Evanses had had the same idea, furnishing their residence with low tables and sectional seating by Gilbert Rohde, a New York–born designer whose work embraced the spirit of the era. The owners

Top Luxuriant plantings almost conceal the green and cream stucco house.

Above The interior is warm and romantic, with a hint of Raymond Chandler and *Chinatown*.

Opposite A fluted mahogany bar adjoins the dining room with its furnishings by Gilbert Rohde.

acquired a Rohde dining table, cabinets, and a kidney-shaped coffee table, which are complemented by a Paul Frankl sofa and a Frankl desk that belonged to the celebrated tenor Lauritz Melchior. The fluted mahogany bar, crafted by Sam Hatch from a design by Jacques-Emile Ruhlmann, is the sole concession to European taste.

The Rabkins continue to refine their collection and make active use of their treasures. The architecture is of its era, but its openness anticipates the informality of our own time. Eric Lloyd Wright served as consulting architect and praises the owners' dedication: "The way they've captured the feeling of what my father was trying to do with space is quite remarkable."

Opposite A contemporary artwork by Charles Arnoldi dominates the restored staircase.

Above In the master bedroom, an angular Paul Frankl screen stands beside the Lloyd Wright–designed bed.

schweikher house-studio

schaumburg, illinois
paul schweikher
1937–38, 1947

In 1937, the long sea voyage from Tokyo to San Francisco gave Paul Schweikher plenty of time to reflect on his first trip to Japan and to remember the modern landmarks he had earlier seen in Europe on a traveling scholarship from Yale. Those experiences shaped his 4,800-square-foot house-studio, which he sketched on the ship and soon built in open country 25 miles northwest of Chicago. He had worked for two well-established architects, David Adler and George Frederick Keck, and had recently formed his own partnership. His fee for remodeling a farm that had formerly concealed one of Al Capone's stills was a seven-acre plot in Roselle, a community founded by German farmers in 1848. Later renamed Schaumburg, it has recently been swallowed up by suburbia, but the house survives in its original condition.

Schweikher's favorite material was wood, and this flat-roofed post-and-beam house is built, inside and out, of California redwood in combination with salmon-colored common brick. Its simplicity is enriched by rough-textured natural materials and inventive details. The Japanese influence is evident in the low ceilings; the integration of rooms, covered porches, and enclosed patios; and the vertical wood screens. There is even a wooden soaking tub, with English-language instructions filched from a Japanese *ryokan* that conclude with the capitalized warning "For heaven's sake, do not take the stopper off the tub bottom!"

As in Japan, there is a processional route. It starts at the carport, moving towards the entry along a raised, covered brick walkway. The walkway is flanked by the blank batten walls of the house and, at an angle, the studio, which together define a grassy courtyard. A low-ceilinged lobby leads into the

Above A gallery linking the living and sleeping areas is lined with closets and opens onto a gravel courtyard.

Opposite In the lofty living room, a massive hearth of end-laid bricks adjoins a dining nook.

50 soaring living room with its brick floor, exposed joists, and huge hearth topped by a wall of end-laid bricks. It is lit from a corner slit and from sliding glass windows opening onto a zen courtyard of raked gravel, with a maple tree that turns scarlet in fall. An all-wood kitchen with open shelves on two sides is linked by a pass-through to a dining nook with a wall bench.

To the right of the lobby is a glass-fronted gallery looking out on the courtyard. The gallery is backed by a wall of closets and a clerestory with wooden flaps to provide cross ventilation. Beyond are the master suite and two additions of 1947: a former child's bedroom with a tiled floor and shoji screen, and a studio with another end-laid brick hearth surround. In 1960, the studio was converted into the children's room, with twin beds cantilevered off a wall bench.

The architect built this residence for himself, but it worked equally well for the couple to whom he sold it in 1953 when he was named chairman of the Yale School of Architecture. Alexander Langsdorf Jr. had come to Chicago to work with nuclear physicist Enrico Fermi on the Manhattan project. He was survived by his wife, Martyl, a celebrated artist who added Eliel Saarinen furniture that she bought a half century ago. She is deeply attached to the house and has turned the architect's office into a studio where she creates paintings that are shown around the world.

FIRST FLOOR

Opposite This children's bedroom with its brick hearth was added by Schweikher in 1947.

Above A raised brick walkway flanks the carport; to the left is the studio with its battened wood walls.

alexander house

silver lake, california
harwell hamilton harris
1940 – 41
restored 1992

It is easy to overlook the houses of Harwell Harris, for, with a few notable exceptions, they are reticent to the point of mystery, and conceal their artistry. Though he quit sculpture class to work with Richard Neutra on the Lovell Health House, an icon of International Modern, Harris always felt closer to the craft tradition of the Japanese and the Greene brothers' California bungalows. He decided to become an architect after his first astonished encounter with Frank Lloyd Wright's Hollyhock house. But the modest residence he designed for the Alexanders is an abstraction of the master's earlier Prairie houses: emphatically horizontal, with a shallow pitched roof, broad eaves, and blank white stucco planes. It is set back behind a walled courtyard and a forecourt that was formed by setting the garage at a right angle to the street.

"We knew nothing about Harris when we bought it, but the house has proved deeply satisfying," say Barry and Jenny Isaacson, a young English couple who are raising a family here. "It's tranquil, light, and pared down to the essentials: we use every inch of it." The Alexanders must have felt the same way—they lived here for 50 years.

Nancy and Kyle Smith, realtors with a passion for modernism, bought it from them and did a major restoration. Over the years, the house had been overlaid with shag rugs and heavy drapes, walls had been papered and covered with pressed tin, and a security grill darkened the living room. These layers were stripped away. Eric Lamers replicated French windows that had been replaced by sliders and reinstalled the triangular baseboard. Straight-grain fir joinery was stained dark brown to restore its original character, and the 1950s kitchen replaced by something closer to the original. Cherokee-red Magnacite was poured to replace disfigured concrete floors.

To understand why this 1,700-square-foot residence feels so spacious and rewarding, one should read Harris's list of nine points to observe in designing a small house, which he compiled in 1935 for *California Arts & Architecture*. Plan the building not as a box with cells, but as a series of partially enclosed spaces, he urges. Do not make rooms serve as halls— keep them apart from traffic flow, and do not crowd too many activities into one room. Group the openings—decide what should be glass and what solid. Accept the fact that light attracts, and give every room a sunny exposure. Make one wall of a room of glass, opening into a walled garden and framed by the roof. Scale the walls of a

Above Pergolas and roof planes extend out over the walled courtyard and complement the white stucco.

Opposite The dining room with its Eliel Saarinen table and chairs and red magnacite floor

room to its floor area. Use the same finishes throughout. And finally, keep the furniture line low and pieces few, light, and movable.

A three-foot module gives the Alexander house a lively rhythm that carries you through a succession of closed and open spaces along axes that shift and turn. There is a sense of transparency in the expansive living room that commands a sweeping view over the canyon to the west, opens onto the patio, and flows into the dining room and adjoining galley kitchen. Cove lighting provides soft ambient illumination. The stairs feel as though they have been carved from a solid block of wood. They carry you up to a tight-knit complex of bedrooms,

each of which opens onto a deck. Harris's signature wood band line leads the eye forward from room to room and acts as a scaling device to reinforce the sense of intimacy.

The Isaacsons have heeded the architect's advice on furniture and have used a restrained palette. An elegant dining table and upholstered chairs by Eliel Saarinen, a Harris Airplane sofa, and a Cloud cork coffee table by Paul Frankl are complemented by thirteen pieces commissioned from Seattle-based designer Roy McMakin, whose wit, craft, and love of nature are a perfect match for those of Harris.

Above The master bedroom opens up to a roof terrace; the bed was designed by Roy McMakin.

Top Harris set the garage at a right angle to the forecourt to minimize its impact to the street.

Opposite The living room is furnished with a mix of new and period pieces and commands a sweeping view over a canyon.

FIRST FLOOR

machines for living

Le Corbusier's vision of the house as "a machine for living" seemed attainable for
a few years at the beginning of the Depression and again at the end of World War II.
The urgent need to revive the economy and provide affordable housing spurred
architects to exploit new techniques and materials and to attempt to harness industry.
Prefabrication and rapid assembly were the goals, but the RV is the only machine for
living that has won wide acceptance. A few steel-framed houses were built and show
what might have been achieved, had the conservatism of the building industry and the
market not impeded mass production.

dymaxion house

dearborn, michigan
buckminster fuller
1945–46
restored by james ashby
1999–2001

The Dymaxion house was one of several early experiments in prefabrication. Another rare survivor is the Aluminaire, which its makers dubbed "a House for Contemporary Life." Designed by the Swiss architect Albert Frey and A. Lawrence Kocher, the editor of *Architectural Record*, the Aluminare was commissioned for the 1931 Allied Arts and Building Products Exhibition in New York and was visited by 100,000 people in a week. A cutaway cube, clad in corrugated aluminum, it was clearly inspired by the Villa Savoye, which Frey had worked on during his brief stint with Le Corbusier in Paris, and that architect's earlier Pavilion de l'Esprit Nouveau. After the exhibition, architect Wallace Harrison bought it to serve as a guesthouse on his Long Island estate; in 1988 it was again disassembled and is currently under restoration on the Islip, Long Island campus of the New York Institute of Technology.

In 1933 George Frederick Keck designed an octagonal "House of Tomorrow" for the Chicago Century of Progress Exposition. A showcase of solar heating, with a central service core and built-in furniture, it also included a hangar for the owner's biplane! The Crystal House, which Keck created for the second year of the fair, was even bolder; its external steel trusses and glass cladding anticipated high-tech buildings of the 1970s.

Few remember these bold visions, but Buckminster Fuller (1895–1983) captured the public imagination through a lifetime of innovation. More inventor than architect, he first conceived his Dymaxion house (he coined the name to stand for *dynamic* and *maximum efficiency*) in 1927. He presented a model at a Chicago department store soon after, but had to wait until 1945 for the opportunity to build it. Alarmed at the prospect of a postwar slump, a union president invited him to present his ideas to the Beech Aircraft Corporation in Wichita, Kansas. The response was enthusiastic.

The cylindrical Dymaxion house was 36 feet in diameter and 22 feet high, a structure inspired by trees and umbrellas. The steel deck and roof canopy were cantilevered out like branches from a trunk of stainless steel tubes that were rooted in concrete. The skin of aluminum sections was bolted to a cage of steel rods and compression rings and braced with cables. A rotating ventilator evacuated hot air and could be cranked up three feet to relieve internal pressure during a tornado. None of the 3,600 parts weighed more than ten pounds. They could be shipped to the site in a cylinder and erected by

Opposite The sole Dymaxion house to be completed as it appeared in 1948 on an estate near Wichita, Kansas

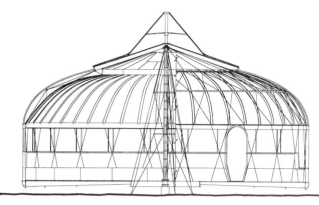

ELEVATION

six workers in a day at a cost of $6,500. Built-ins included five metal units with rotating shelves and racks, a closet with pivoting storage for clothes and shoes, and an all-in-one bathroom unit.

Life magazine published photos of a cozily furnished interior, mocked up in the factory, and 37,000 orders flooded in. A corporation was formed to begin production and its stock soared, but Fuller felt more time was needed to perfect the design, and the delay proved fatal. William Graham, a stockholder in the company, bought the two prototypes for $2,000 and combined them on his estate in Wichita. There the structure ended its life as a swinging bachelor pad for USAF pilots.

In 1992, the house was acquired by the Henry Ford Museum and Greenfield Village, which did extensive research and later hired architectural conservator James Ashby to supervise the house's restoration and re-assembly within its galleries. Ashby strives for aesthetic integrity, and draws on the expertise of the museum staff as well as his own research on aluminum conservation. The prototypes were slightly different, so adjustments have to be made in combining the salvageable 75 percent of original parts with replicas, and adding features (like a neoprene gutter) that were designed but never installed. Exposure to the sun changed the temper of the metal, and the

cladding exfoliated, so surviving pieces have been heat-treated to stabilize the crystalline structure of the alloy.

The douglas fir ply sectional floorboards were cleaned, plugged, and shellacked. A draped ceiling canopy of parachute silk, which was sucked out through the ventilator by a tornado, will be replaced. Every rib and bolt has to be cleaned or fabricated, and judgments made about the furnishing of a house that was never used as Fuller intended. The restoration is as challenging as was the original design and the structure is, as of this writing, on display as a work in progress.

The Aluminaire house is located beside the Sunburst Building on the NYIT Islip campus. Information: (631) 348-3363; http://www.nyit.edu. The Henry Ford Museum is located at 20900 Oakwood Boulevard, Dearborn, and is open 9am–5pm, except on Thanksgiving and Christmas Day. Information: (313) 271-1620; http://www.hfmgv.org.

Opposite The Aluminaire house of 1931, currently under restoration at the New York Institute of Technology on Long Island

Right Reassembling the Dymaxion house, during the lengthy restoration process at the Henry Ford Museum in Michigan

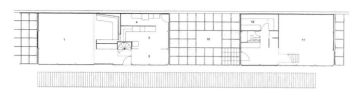

SECOND FLOOR

FIRST FLOOR

eames
house-studio

62

pacific palisades, california
charles & ray eames
1948–49

The 1,500-square-foot house that the Eameses built for themselves on a meadow looking out to the ocean is an expression of Charles's fascination with problem solving and technology, infused with Ray's passion for color, pattern, and detail. It is a work of art, entirely composed of parts ordered from builders' catalogues and efficiently assembled: a machine with a soul. Photographs—of a structural frame assembled in a day, a Mondrian-like grid of black

steel and glass with colored infill panels as accents, and a soaring interior filled with prototype furniture and objects the couple had collected from around the world—brought the house immediate fame and continue to inspire other architects.

The couple were living in a Richard Neutra apartment when they first conceived the house as a steel-framed, single-story structure cantilevered from a hillside and supported on slender columns. That scheme was published as Case Study House #8 in *Arts + Architecture,* together with #9, an Eero Saarinen house across the meadow for the magazine's publisher, John Entenza. Delays caused by shortages of building materials allowed the Eameses to rethink the design

and create double-height volumes with the same amount of steel. "It is interesting to consider how the rigidity of the system was responsible for the free use of space," wrote Charles, "and to see how the most matter of fact structure resulted in pattern and texture."

The Eames's 1955 film, *House: After Five Years of Living*, shows a magical space that opens up to nature. It absorbs the sunlight filtering in through translucent panels and the young eucalyptus trees that have now grown to dwarf the house. In those early years, the interior was still evolving, as the private retreat of two extraordinary designers, shared only with a few fortunate friends and associates. Charles died in 1978

and Ray followed ten years later to the day; the life of the house was extinguished then, and the contents were frozen in time. Today, it is a beautiful relic, cherished by Charles's daughter, Lucia, and by her son, Eames Demetrios, who uses the studio and is finding new ways to re-animate the house while preserving it as Ray left it.

The Eames house is located at 203 Chautauqua Boulevard, Pacific Palisades, California. The exterior may be viewed by appointment, and occasional fundraising tours of the interior are offered. Information: (310) 396-5991; http://www.eames.com.

Opposite The house and, beyond, the studio are entirely composed from parts ordered out of builders' catalogues.

Left The entry frames a spiral stair and is itself framed by towering eucalyptus trees.

Opposite The lofty living room and an intimate sitting area tucked in below the bedroom balcony

morris house

silverlake, california
allyn e. morris
1955–58
restored 1998–99

The Bauhaus ideal of combining handicraft with the machine is perfectly expressed in this extraordinary hillside house. A mosaic-trimmed canopy of white stucco floats over a brick-paved carport and a translucent glass entry. Beyond this enigmatic façade is a taut, spare glass box overlooking a canyon. The drama of the structure and the view is enhanced by the beauty of its component parts. Both the delicate steel frame and the springy spiral stair

linking sleeping, living, and work spaces are painted primary red. Slim concrete slabs are cut away from the frame, allowing space to flow around them, and counterweighted windows slide up, opening the living room onto a cantilevered deck. Floor planes and fanned stair treads are edged in turquoise glass mosaic, which is also used in the kitchen, in the bathroom, and on the patterned brick piers. There is even an accent of gold (a single mosaic square on each tread), and the tubular counterweights are yellow. But this playful ornament is integrated with a functional design, in which a few materials are honestly exposed.

"Dixieland is a passion of mine and I was trying to make jazz in this house," says Allyn

Morris, an architect who studied engineering at Stanford and moved to Los Angeles in 1950. "The module is two by four feet and that provides a rhythm. Like the beat in jazz it holds the whole thing together." Morris wanted his house to be as practical as possible, making the carport wide for easy access off a narrow street, putting the dressing area just inside the entry for a quick change out of work clothes, and setting the bed high on a brick pier so he would not have to bend over to make it. The steel was assembled in three days, but he moved in with his new wife, Mary, before the glass was installed, and it took several years of sweat and scraping up money to complete the house. A structure

originally designed for an athletic bachelor was no place to raise a small child: in 1962, when their son Howard was born, they moved out.

Luckily, after a long period of abuse (neighbors still gossip about the steamy parties), the house was refurbished by Nancy Smith and sold to an aficionado.

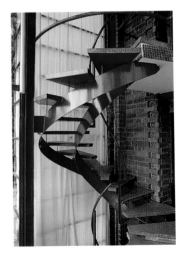

Opposite A taut, spare box bracketed by cantilevered concrete planes that extend out from a steep hillside

Top A mosaic-trimmed canopy of white stucco juts over a brick-paved carport and recessed entrance.

Above A steel spiral stair with concrete treads links the three levels of the house.

Stephen Chin was studying law at Yale and discovering architecture through the lectures of Vincent Scully when he first saw this house. He bought it in 1994, soon after moving to Los Angeles to produce independent features. "I'm the kind of person this house was designed for," Chin says. "At first I thought of extending it, but the longer I stayed, the more it offered me. It imposed a kind of rigor in my life, and, as soon as I made some money, I decided to restore it. You have to ask yourself: what makes the house work? What are the elements of its personality? If I'd dashed ahead, I'd have made many mistakes; instead, I waited five years, then spent months talking to Morris. I invited him down to

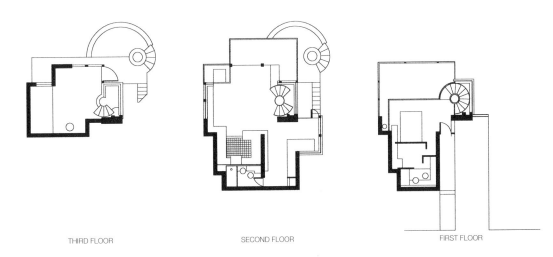

THIRD FLOOR   SECOND FLOOR   FIRST FLOOR

Opposite Counterweighted windows slide up, opening the living room to the projected terrace.

Above Classic Eames seating in a corner of the living room

Opposite "Dixieland is a passion of mine and I was trying to make jazz in this house," recalls the architect.

Above New kitchen cabinets and a ceiling grille respect the spirit of the original design.

participate in a local support group of modern homeowners who shared tips on restoration. He was gratified by the respect he received, and unearthed all the original plans."

Though the plan is open and light floods in from every side, each area has its own character. In the bedroom, Chin has added drapes so that he is not woken at sunrise. The studio area, opening onto a brick garden terrace, serves as a quiet sanctuary that could double as a guest bedroom. Most of the improvements have been made at the mid level. The owner loves to cook Chinese but decided that a contemporary kitchen, opening into the living room, would be jarring. Instead, working with restoration contractor Eric Lammers, he tried to reconstruct the original, respecting the alternation of high and low cabinets and facing them with red laminate that matches the steel. He replaced the mirror on the rear wall, which enlarges the space and catches the lights of the city, and he installed aluminum grid ceiling panels, which diffuse fluorescent and reflect natural light, in place of the original honeycomb plastic. In the bathroom, the lip of the shower tray was raised to create a soaking tub, using vintage 1950s tile. In his attention to detail, and his spare use of mid-century furniture, lighting, and glassware, Chin has recreated an architect's dream and fulfilled his own.

73

Opposite Jacobsen chairs, a Noguchi table, and a Nelson lamp in the compact dining area

Above As in the Gropius house, the stair rails complement the orthogonal geometry of the windows.

Top The platform bed is set high on a brick pier, suspended within the light-filled volume of the house.

case study house #21

hollywood, california
pierre koenig
1958 – 59
restored, 1997 – 98

For Pierre Koenig, "steel is a way of life, not something you pick up or put down." He has stayed true to his principles ever since he defied his instructors at the University of Southern California School of Architecture and built a steel-framed bungalow for himself in 1950. His mentor, Raphael Soriano, and other men of steel, such as Mies and Ellwood, are gone, but Koenig is unwaveringly rigorous in his practice. Yet his reputation is largely sustained by an iconic

image of the 1960 Case Study House #22. Julius Shulman immortalized the house in his nighttime photograph of two women in white conversing within a glass-walled living room that is cantilevered out above a magic carpet of lights. In contrast to that dramatic structure, this earlier house seems almost Japanese in its austerity and restraint.

Outside and in, it is a minimalist, monochromatic box. An exposed steel frame supports a flat steel deck, windowless steel walls to east and west, and sliding glass walls to north and south. Water spouts from gutters into a moat that reflects light onto the walls and ceiling and is recycled back. Brick terraces extend to the north and

south, and the frame embraces a double carport. Koolshade (micro-louver sliding screens) on the south face provide shade in summer and can be removed in winter for passive solar heating. The structural columns and beams are painted charcoal,

establishing a modular rhythm within the all-white interior. Living areas and two bedrooms are separated by a central core of bathrooms and mechanical services, clad with blue mosaic tiles and divided by a light well that is open to the sky. The pure lines,

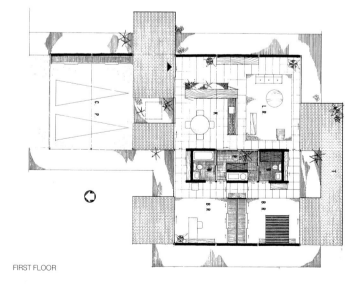

FIRST FLOOR

Opposite Water spouts from a gutter into the moat and is recycled.

precise geometry, and expanses of white (Koenig refuses to countenance pictures on his bare walls) heighten the impact of the plantings and throw every object into sharp relief.

Walter Bailey, a leading psychotherapist, and his wife, Mary, chose the site because this was a cooperative housing project that actively fostered modern architecture, disallowing picket fences and shingled roofs, and was one of only two racially unrestricted developments in Los Angeles. The project was launched by four musicians after the war. Incredible as it now seems, their liberal policy was contested by the city, the Department of Housing and Urban Development, and the Federal Housing Authority, all the way to the U.S. Supreme Court, which finally granted an exception to the racist policies of that time. The Baileys told Koenig to do what he wanted as long as it cost no more than $22,000, but then spent a year struggling to secure a mortgage.

The house survived the neglect of subsequent owners in shabby but structurally sound condition. It was bought in 1997 by Dan Craccioli, who coproduced *The Matrix;* he commissioned Koenig to restore it to its pristine condition. Work stretched out over eighteen months, twice what it took for construction, so frustrating was the quest for original materials and so exacting the replacement

Above Sliding window walls open the living area to the south terrace.

Top Approached over a moat, this all-steel house has a Japanese austerity and restraint.

Opposite Entry court and kitchen: an alternation of opaque and transparent planes

of mechanical elements and lighting. New white vinyl floor tiles and bathroom mosaics were installed, together with kitchen appliances scaled to the long-vanished originals. Bathroom doors gave way to sliders of translucent laminated glass, and bedroom mirrors to sliding screens of masonite. A fountain will be added, as originally intended, in the light well. "There was a weird sense of deja vu after 40 years," says the architect, "but also a wonderful feeling about getting it right again."

Craccioli needed more than 1,320 square feet and has commissioned a larger house from Koenig. The new owner of the house, actor Michael Fettes, matches Craccioli's enthusiasm. "I grew up in a 1960s house and was always interested in technologies that made living simpler," he explains. "This house is functional without a lot of fuss, and it makes you live within reasonable constraints—like a vacation cabin—though I do have another house in Malibu. When I moved to California I said I would take only what I could carry, and though I didn't stick to that, this house allows me to feel I did. It's my fortress of solitude, out in nature, yet close to the center of town."

Opposite Exposed black beams and white decking are used throughout the house.

Above View from the open kitchen into the dining area

Top The carport is treated as another room in the house.

embracing the landscape

Frank Lloyd Wright and his protegés, as well as architects who pursued a radically different course, shared a love of nature and made it an integral part of their compositions. The houses discussed here, as well as many in other sections, demonstrate the interdependence of sharp-edged buildings and organic plantings—what Richard Neutra called "the machine in the garden."

weston havens house

berkeley, california
harwell hamilton harris
1939 – 41

In her brilliant biography of Harwell Harris, Lisa Germany suggests that his early clients "did not care to show the world that they were up to date," and shared "a complete absence of pretense . . . a desire to lose oneself in a house that was itself lost in nature . . . an intense yearning for seclusion and repose." Weston Havens, a bachelor and heir to a San Francisco Bay–area land fortune, felt that way. "I had seen Harwell's work illustrated in magazines and particularly liked his own house, even though it was only twelve feet square," the nonagenarian recalls. "He didn't have a degree, and when people started complaining he had stationery printed with 'Not an Architect' at the head. We met, I invited him to the site and told him I wanted walls that were either glass or bookshelves." Harris sketched, made a clay model of a house stacked up against a steep hillside, and completed it the week before the attack on Pearl Harbor. He was helped by Walter Stauberg, a local architect who had worked with the Beaux Arts architect Julia Morgan. The house has survived several earthquakes and has aged gracefully while remaining remarkably close to its original condition.

The pine trees Havens planted 60 years ago have blocked the house's dramatic profile: it has three inverted gables that Germany likens to "upturned hat brims." All that is visible from the street is a wide carport and a slatted wood gate. The gate opens onto an enclosed wood stair. This leads down to a V-section bridge with pivoting glass louvers that crosses the inner courtyard (formerly a badminton court) to the main level of the house. Unsealed redwood cladding has bleached in the sun and darkened in the shade. It is easy to imagine yourself in a temple in Kyoto until the panorama of Berkeley, bay, and sky comes into view, framed by a ceiling that tilts up from seven feet at the bookshelves to fifteen feet at the rim. Cement board is nailed to trusses on the underside of the ceiling—a cladding anticipated by Bernard Maybeck in his Christian Science church of 1910 in Berkeley. The wedge section vault doubles as a truss and a plenum chamber with hot air vents and also admits indirect natural and fluorescent light through glass panels in the ceiling.

Living and dining areas open up through a window wall to a broad terrace. A beveled concrete mantel over the hearth echoes the profile of the ceiling vault and reflects heat. A pass-through that can be masked by doors painted with a map of the world links the dining area to a spacious kitchen that is far

Opposite The terrace commands a sweeping view of Berkeley and the San Francisco Bay.

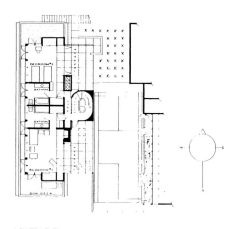

LOWER LEVEL

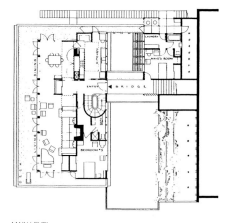

MAIN LEVEL

Opposite The living room is lit from window walls to the left and a concealed skylight to the right.

Above Space flows freely from one end of the house to the other, linking the major living areas.

Above Alvar Aalto's linoleum-topped dining table and webbed chairs have survived six decades.

87

ahead of its time. Broad lighting channels run around the perimeter and high central ceiling, illuminating some of the earliest built-in ovens and aluminum work surfaces. A corridor curves around the stairwell to a guest bedroom, and a tightly wound spiral stair with birch plywood paneling leads down to the modestly scaled master bedroom, another guest room, and out into the landscaped courtyard. Services and storage occupy the level below that.

Construction took over a year. Havens recalls that "the window frames were made off site and trucked up. Some were broken in transit, others wouldn't fit. There's no conventional molding so they had to be exact. No one could supply panes of glass that were large enough to fill the tall windows, so there's a break at the bottom. I told Harwell what I wanted for furnishings and many were built in." These were supplemented with Scandinavian modern pieces, such as the extendable, linoleum-topped Aalto dining table, and some postwar additions. An artist did the Patrician blue walls, and the original sailcloth drapes were replaced with matchstick blinds.

Harris was indifferent to architectural fashions, and this treasure will never go out of style. As with the Eames house, it is a timeless work of art that expresses the personalities of its owner and designer.

Opposite The house is entered over the Japanese-style bridge that crosses the inner courtyard.

Above Three inverted gables form a distinctive profile that is now concealed by foliage.

Top Open-sided bridge leading to the entry of the house

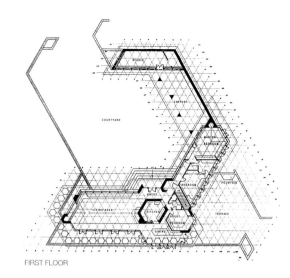

FIRST FLOOR

kentuck knob

chalkhill, pennsylvania
frank lloyd wright
1953–56
restored by robert s. taylor &
richard cleary
1986–88

I.N. Hagan distributed milk from the dairy herd of Edgar Kaufmann, who invited him up to Fallingwater and inspired him to commission a Wright house for his own family. "Offer him half what you are prepared to pay since it's sure to cost twice as much," Kaufmann advised. The architect studied photos of the site, which was 2,000 feet up on a steep wooded hillside, and mailed plans. Hagan requested higher ceilings to suit his six-foot son, a living room twice as long

as the one planned, and stone-paved floors—rejecting the architect's choice of concrete as was fit only for hog barns. These improvements, and the high quality construction—including double-stone cavity walls and meticulous detailing—pushed the price of the 2,200-square-foot house to $96,000.

Though Wright did not visit the site until the floor was being laid, the house is an inspired response to the beauty of the landscape. A sharp stone prow, boldly modeled like the wall of a quarry, rises from the bottom of slope, and a pierced and chambered wood canopy sails above it. The monumentality of the base contrasts with the welcoming scale of the graveled entry court, enclosed on five sides by

ground-hugging living and sleeping wings, the office-carport, and a low retaining wall. A hexagonal masonry kitchen and chimney rise above the stepped copper roofs as the symbolic hub of the house. This geometric form is echoed in the courtyard and the 72 openings that cast pools of light (and piles of snow in winter) through the canopy onto the stone-flagged terrace.

Low-rise stone steps lead up to glass entry doors. The interior is full of dramatic contrasts, and every space flows out on a diagonal. There is a great sense of lightness and openness beyond the shallow, low-ceilinged hall that compels a sharp turn into the spacious, lofty living room, with its steel-framed pitched

ceiling vault. An eight-foot-high soffit on either side creates a sense of intimacy at the periphery of this grand volume. At the far end, glass is set directly into the stone, bisecting a planter and obliterating the divide between indoors and out. Throughout, Wright played up the contrast of solid and transparent, from the massive stone hearth to the glass doors that open onto the terrace. The clerestory is masked by a fretted wood screen, and flaps can be opened to provide cross ventilation.

The architect asserted his love of intimacy in the private areas of the house. In the snug, skylit kitchen, with its wood cabinets and early 1950s appliances are ranged round stone walls and a cork floor. In contrast, the

Opposite Hexagonal openings in the cantilevered roof plane cast pools of light on the stone-flagged terrace.

dining room projects out onto the terrace and is walled with glass on three sides, putting diners amid the tree tops. Three cavelike bedrooms with 21-inch-wide door openings are reached by a narrow corridor lined with shelves. Angled walls, triangular stone piers, vaulted ceilings, and tiny bathrooms complement the built-in beds and generous closets. To reinforce the feeling of enclosure, windows are placed to direct your eyes toward the ground.

The Hagans enjoyed the house for 35 years. When they left, though, it proved hard to find a buyer in this remote, economically depressed area, a 90-minute drive from Pittsburgh. In 1986, Lord Palumbo learned Kentuck Knob was for sale while visiting Fallingwater, immediately drove to see it, and purchased it on a second visit for $600,000. Soon after, a fire caused by farm equipment destroyed the studio, the carport, and half the bedroom wing, with heavy smoke damage to other areas. Robert Taylor, a Pittsburgh architect, and consulting architectural historian Richard Cleary directed the reconstruction and cleaning, working from photographs, Wright's drawings, and memories of those who knew the house. There was no more freestone on the estate, but they found similar stone in a demolished barn and were also able to match the tidewater red cypress. A new copper roof was installed with improved ventilation and fire-stops in the crawl spaces,

Left The low, ground-hugging bedroom wing extends from the hexagonal stone tower of the kitchen.

Above Vaulted ceilings rise above this living space, along the side of which runs a long bench. A stone hearth can be seen in the background.

and the skylight over the dining room was made weather-tight.

Palumbo makes regular visits, and has bought a nearby farmhouse where he can stay with his family, strolling over to enjoy the house and to sleep there on Sunday nights (there are no public tours on Mondays). To give the house a new vitality, he has juxtaposed furniture by Wright and other modern masters with colorful kilims, Warhol flower paintings, and silver-framed photos of family and friends. And he has enhanced the landscape by inviting Andy Galsworthy, Ray Smith, and other artists to install site-specific sculpture among the trees.

Kentuck Knob is located six miles from Fallingwater. Tours are offered 10am–4pm, Tuesday–Sunday. Information: (724) 329-1901; http://www.kentuckknob.com.

Opposite A sharp stone prow, boldly modeled like the wall of a quarry, rises from the bottom of the slope.

Above, left The lofty living room achieves a balance of grandeur and intimacy, mass and transparency

Above, right The massive stone hearth and kitchen constitute the symbolic hub of the house.

Top The entry court is enclosed on five sides by the house, office-carport, and low retaining walls.

villa ponte

new canaan, connecticut
john m. johansen
1956–57

"This house represented a rediscovery of the Renaissance through the villas of Palladio," recalls John Johansen, "even though I shared the moderns' faith that the past has no hold on us. At school I was hugely enthusiastic about German modern, but Ulrich Franzen and I wanted to break out of the Bauhaus box. We had unbounded energy and curiosity to explore different possibilities." In the early 1940s Johansen was part of the first wave of graduates from the reformed Harvard GSD, and later married Walter Gropius's daughter, but he has been exploring the outer frontiers of modernism for more than 50 years. Even as he built white boxes and paraphrased Palladio, he was creating organic structures of sprayed concrete. "I find romance and poetry in the most extraordinary technology," says this irrepressible octogenarian, citing experiments to "grow" houses through molecular engineering.

His clients moved to New Canaan in the mid-1950s, when the area was mission central for modernism. They decided they could not afford Philip Johnson, and chose Johansen. A stream ran through the leafy site, and the architect tried fifteen different

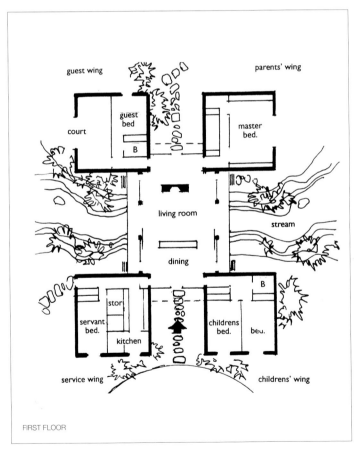

FIRST FLOOR

Top Four stucco pavilions are linked by a bridge with arched roof shells that spans a stream.

Opposite A rock pool beside the stream emphasizes the delicacy and precision of the house.

ways of capturing its beauty. He won acceptance for a romantic, but rigorously symmetrical, scheme of four coral-pink stucco pavilions, linked by a bridge over the water that contains the foyer and the living and dining rooms. Master and guest bedrooms occupy the front pavilions; kitchen and service areas and childrens' bedrooms, those in back. Two steel beams support a 55-foot-long concrete slab spanning the water; steel posts and beams bear lightweight arched roof shells; and the glass walls frame views up and down the stream. This suggests a cross axis that complements the progression from the recessed entry to a similar court at the rear, opening onto forest, and tying the house into the landscape.

The poetry is in the details. A white cornice line links the five volumes, and the stucco of each block is randomly stamped with a different motif. Rainwater that collects on the flat roofs reflects light onto the gold-leafed soffits of the arches, and is carried away through bronze gargoyles. A polished terrazzo floor also mirrors the play of light and evokes the serenity of a classic Italian villa. A hearth of speckled brick divides the living room from the foyer, and a freestanding black closet does the same for the dining room at the far end. The 3,500-square-foot house has been maintained in impeccable condition and continues to delight the owners when they return every spring from their winter retreat in Florida.

Above An alternation of solid and void breaks up the mass of the house and provides framed views of the landscape.

Top Pavers set in gravel lead to the entry, establishing an axis that flows through the house and out on the far side.

Opposite, top The formal arrangement of the living room contrasts with the airy gold-leafed arches of the vault.

Opposite The dining table appears to float on the polished terrazzo floor and is bathed in natural light from three sides.

straus house

pound ridge, new york
edward larrabee barnes
1957–59

Edward Barnes was a contemporary of Johansen's at Harvard. He has stayed closer to the mainstream of American modernism, alternating between large urban projects, such as the Walker Art Center in Minneapolis and the IBM tower in Manhattan, and rural retreats that merge into the landscape. His own house at Mount Kisco, New York, built in 1952 and subsequently added to, is a white object on a platform, raised above the land. But a later commission for John Straus, an old school friend, took him over a year to design, so anxious was he to respect the beauty of the rocky, wooded site bordered by a still pond. "I wondered if I should build there and took so long that they began to worry about me," Barnes recalls. "Luckily, they were model clients, helped shape the house and kept it in wonderful condition. It remains one of my favorites."

Though it has withstood 40 winters, the house is occupied only in summer, allowing the architect to break up the 4,000 square feet into four discrete volumes, reducing the mass, defining courtyards and opening every room up to nature and cross ventilation. On plan, the geometry is Miesian. The

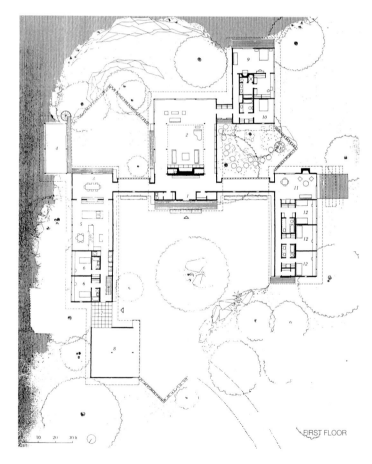

FIRST FLOOR

10   20   30 ft

Opposite The master bedroom wing is raised on slender posts above the gently sloping ground.

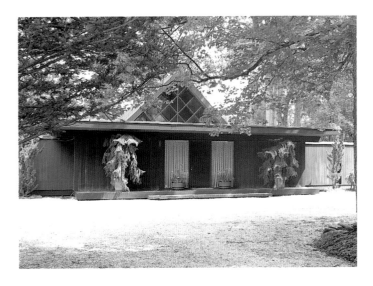

Above Low wings extend into the wooded landscape and the screen porch is raised on posts above the pond.

Top The pitch-vaulted living room rises above the entry hall that links the two side wings of the house.

102

children's and master bedrooms to the west, and the service areas, dining room, and screen porch to the east, seem to slide past the great room at the center, with a cross-axial corridor at the front and glazed galleries to tie them together. Close up, the house evokes a Japanese flavor in the insistent horizontality of its black-stained cedar boards, especially where they frame the gleaming white gravel of the entrance court. Where the ground dips, the structure is raised on pilotis, and the screen porch is lofted over the water for alfresco candlelit dinners undisturbed by bugs.

Garden courts are partly enclosed by angled stone walls. These echo the pitched vault of the great room, which anchors

the low wings and pulls in light through its stained glass gables. A massive hearth, its handsome masonry sparkling with flecks of mica, strengthens this central focus. Polished tiles catch light from the expansive windows, but the trees cut out much of the sun, making the interior a cool, shady escape from the heat of summer—a refreshing retreat after a picnic on the lawn or a dip in the pond.

Above A stone hearth that sparkles from specks of mica and a colored glass window add richness to the great room.

Top Intimate, simply furnished rooms serve as a cool retreat from the heat of the summer.

Opposite The screen porch juts out over the pond and provides an ideal setting for summer entertaining.

secular temples

Ever since the Renaissance, the classical monuments of the Mediterranean have decisively shaped Western architecture. Even the moderns, who rebelled against the Beaux-Arts tradition of symmetrical plans, solid masonry, and pedimented façades, found inspiration in the serene and ideally proportioned structures of ancient Greece and Rome. Employing steel and concrete in place of marble, stripping ornament, and dissolving the wall planes, they created houses of timeless strength and beauty.

farnsworth house

plano, illinois
mies van der rohe
1946–51
restored by dirk lohan
1973–74 / 1997–98

An image of the Farnsworth house captured the imagination of Peter Palumbo while he was still a schoolboy at Eton, and it is easy to sense the "aura of high romance" that inspired him to buy it, 20 years later. As with the Petit Trianon at Versailles, it is an elegant white pavilion set in an idyllic landscape—but it also evokes a Greek temple in its iconic simplicity and harmonious proportions. As it emerges through the trees, it appears to levitate above the emerald meadow that borders the Fox River. Steps lead up to a stage-like platform and up again to the portico of the house, which is set on a raised 77-by-28-foot deck. The travertine floor slabs express the module of 33-by-24 inches. Space flows around a linear service core, with a bathroom at either end dividing a narrow kitchen from a spacious living area. The dining and study areas flank the entrance and a sleeping area occupies the far end. Each wall frames a landscape. All is order, calm, and beauty, yet the house has a turbulent history.

Dr. Edith Farnsworth commissioned the house, then quarreled bitterly with Mies on the eve of completion. Each sued the other. The house was soon damaged in a flood, and the portico was retrofitted with mesh screens to combat the summer plague of mosquitoes. Farnsworth grew to hate the house and moved to Italy in the late 1960s. Palumbo recalls his purchase as "entirely serendipitous." In 1968, he was visiting Chicago to discuss the office tower Mies had designed for a key site in London's financial district. "I happened to arrive early, picked up the *Chicago Tribune* and saw a classified ad for the house—I think it was the first time it had run. When I called, Dr. Farnsworth was there; I told her who I was and asked if I could come out right away." Palumbo knew immediately that he had to have the house, but it

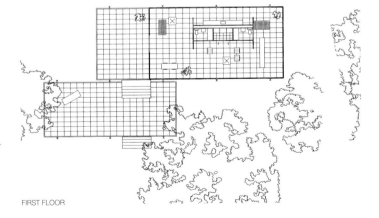

FIRST FLOOR

Opposite An image of this house captured the imagination of Lord Palumbo while he was still a schoolboy in England.

took four years to conclude the deal—by which time Mies had died and his design for London had been rejected by the planning authorities.

Dirk Lohan, Mies's grandson and close associate, supervised a major restoration. The roof was replaced, the screens on the portico removed, and the columns were sandblasted and given multiple coats of white lacquer. To make the house habitable year-round, air conditioning was installed and the heating system and other mechanical services upgraded. Dr. Farnsworth had made her own choice of furnishings—though she asked a student of Mies to design the teak armoire that screens the bedroom from the living room. Lohan designed a Miesian platform bed, dining table, and desk, and replaced roller blinds with white linen-cotton drapes—close to the architect's preference for silk shantung.

Disaster struck again in July 1996, when the river attained record heights. A torrent of muddy water and debris smashed windows and inundated the house to a depth of almost five feet above the five-foot platform that was supposed to protect it. The travertine was cleaned, but the wood panels on the central core had begun to buckle and had to be replaced. A concealed fragment revealed that the Primavera (white mahogany) veneer was much lighter than Lohan had supposed, for the original had been stained and had darkened after frequent applications of linseed oil. A long search (for

Previous spread An elegant white pavilion set in an idyllic landscape, evoking a Greek temple in its iconic simplicity

Above Steps lead up to a low platform and up again to the portico of the house.

Opposite In the office area to the right of the entry resides this desk designed by Dirk Lohan.

113

supplies of Primavera are now almost exhausted) yielded a good match; new drapes were installed; and a mix of new and vintage modern furniture replaced those pieces that could not be restored. The interior is closer now to Mies's intentions than it has ever been. Each piece, each composition, conforms to an aesthetic as rigorous as that of the house, as do the sculptures the owner has placed in the landscape designed by Lanning Roper.

Palumbo has bought an 1850s house nearby for his family, and visits his prize acquisition as though it were were a garden pavilion, to smoke a cigar and soak up the atmosphere. But he has put his stamp on the interior, bringing to odd corners some of the traditional clutter of an English country house. Two umbrella stands bulge with impedimenta, and the bathrooms boast a dense collage of photos and art (plus a framed letter from 10 Downing Street, in which Margaret Thatcher thanks him for his support "at this difficult time"). There is an alarm system to warn of impending floods and the new wall panels can be easily removed. However, the best hope of averting a future catastrophe may be Lohan's audacious proposal to place the house on hydraulic jacks that would raise it seven feet in an emergency.

Tours of the house, a 90-minute drive southwest of Chicago, are offered 10am–4pm, Thursday–Tuesday. Information: (630) 552-8622; http://www.farnsworthhouse.com.

Opposite Space flows around a linear service core that contains services and bathrooms.

Above The sparely furnished living room is framed by window walls and Primavera paneling.

Top A teak armoire conceals the bedroom from the living room.

boissonnas house

new canaan, connecticut
philip johnson
1955–56
restored 1998

Philip Johnson practiced the modernist gospel he had earlier preached for barely a decade, from the Glass House of 1949 to his collaboration with Mies on the Seagram Building, but he created a third masterpiece in this nobly proportioned villa of brick, steel, and glass. The grand central pavilion and low side wings suggest an abstraction of a villa by Palladio or Schinkel, as does the embrace of the formal gardens, the refinement of materials, the spatial richness, and the extraordinary play of light within. A stately succession of brick piers support white steel beams and gridded trellises, which define the stepped entry and shade the master bedroom terrace. Every detail bespeaks quality, from the broad copper coping to the precision with which the black steel frames are set into the impeccably pointed brick. Projecting piers give the house a weight and depth lacking in Johnson's other local work.

The house had one critical flaw: the huge expanses of single glazing made it torrid in summer, and icy in winter. Eric Boissonnas had commissioned the 4,400-square-foot house at the suggestion of Dominique de Menil, Johnson's patron in Houston. He and his wife stayed long enough to add motorized exterior blinds that deflected the sun but disfigured the windows. Six subsequent owners, ending with decorator Jay Spectre, who stayed twelve years and died here after a long illness, made more changes. By 1997, the house had been empty for three years and smelled like it. Heavy drapes blocked the light, the roof leaked, and the garden was overgrown with poison ivy and plentifully littered with dog droppings. For Bill Matassoni, a management consultant, and his wife Pamela Valentine, an attorney, it was love at first sight.

Opposite The living room is a nobly proportioned glass-walled cube.

Above Brick piers support a white trellis above the entrance court.

Overleaf The central pavilion and side wings evoke villas by Palladio and Schinkel.

FIRST FLOOR

119

"We arrived on a freezing December day, spent ten hours closing the deal, and slept on a mattress on the floor," recalls Matassoni. "It took us four months to bring the house back to its original condition." He served as contractor, installing a new roof membrane, replacing all the glass with thermopane, repainting, and clearing the landscape. A vast boiler that filled an entire room in the basement was replaced by a small computer-controlled model, with a second as back-up.

Today the house works and looks as its architect intended. The living room, a near cube, holds its own with the great salons of earlier centuries. It shows how a mastery of scale and materials can provide a sense of warmth and splendor without recourse to ornament or elaborate furnishings. The brick paving, sealed and waxed within, flows out through the glass to the terraces. Classic modern furniture is strategically deployed in island groupings on seagrass rugs, the wall cabinets and hearth surround are of bleached ash, and two trees in copper pots reach up towards a pair of black and gold Japanese screens. There is a dramatic shift from this soaring space to the Mies-furnished dining room with its Byzantine mosaic of a leaping deer. The slate-floored kitchen is spacious; the bedrooms and study are understated and intimate. It is a house that offers a soothing retreat for a busy couple and a stage on which to entertain.

Opposite A sense of warmth and splendor without recourse to ornament or elaborate furnishings

Above A mosaic of a leaping deer hangs on the wall of the Mies-furnished dining room.

Top The breakfast area flows out of the spacious slate-paved kitchen.

lee house #2

new canaan, connecticut
john black lee
1956
enhanced by toshiko mori
1991 – 92

John Black Lee was one of the pioneer modernists of New Canaan. He moved there in 1950 to work with Marcel Breuer, instead found a job with Eliot Noyes, and then launched his own practice. "Modern was more spirit than style in the 'fifties," he recalls. "We all shared the same philosophy, went to the same parties, and felt it was a great thing to build for the common man. But adventurous clients were always uncommon and soon had to be

rich to build here." Lee demonstrated that building could be done at minimal expense in the three houses he constructed for himself over 40 years.

The second was this elegant homage to Mies, nestled on a wooded 20-acre plot (which he bought when land was cheap, selling off much of it to kindred spirits). A symmetrical 2,000-square-foot, rectilinear pavilion,

it comprises an open central area flanked on two sides by pairs of small bedrooms separated by skylit bathrooms. Plywood cabinets enclose the kitchen, also lit from above, which divides the foyer from the living-dining area. A projecting roof plane extends over a veranda on all four sides.

The house's simplicity was the drawing card for Susan

Leaming, who sells contemporary Latin American art, and her banker husband, Eric Pollish. When they bought the house in 1990, they had already found an architect, Toshiko Mori, who shared their minimalist aesthetic. Realizing that Lee might be reluctant to change his own house, they invited Mori to make improvements. It was an ideal choice, for the Japanese-born

Above The house is delicate and springy, transparent and reflective—a foil to nature.

Opposite A wide veranda surrounds the house, offering protection from heat and rain.

Above The original single-glazed sliding windows were replaced with thermopane and pivoting glass doors.

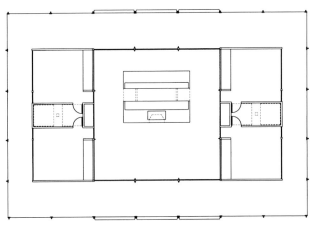

FIRST FLOOR

architect was on the faculty of Cooper Union and had a practice in New York.

"I wanted to respect the character and proportions of the house, while giving it more height and light," Mori explains. She spent six months refining her plan to raise the roof eighteen inches and insert a clerestory; she would also replace the single-glazed sliding windows with thermopane set into slender stainless steel frames and pivoting glass doors. The old glass was installed in the detached garage, making it a memento of the original house. A new glass skylight replaced the Plexiglas bubble over the kitchen—an improvement the owners reprised when they remodeled the bathrooms. To strengthen the structure and lengthen its life, slim T-section steel columns were substituted for the peripheral wood posts, which had been eaten away by carpenter ants. Screens can be installed to make the veranda usable in summer and extend the boundary of the house. The owners may invite Mori back to add a delicate glass pavilion on axis with the house and garage.

More than ever, the house is delicate and springy, transparent and reflective: a gentle foil to nature. Seasonal shifts of color and light are the greatest reward of living here; however, as Leaming, the mother of two, admits: "it's important to keep it spare—there's nowhere to hide things."

Left Toshiko Mori added the clerestory, which pulls in natural light and enhances the proportions of the central space.

Opposite The living-dining area is divided from the entry area by low partitions that enclose the kitchen.

towers house

essex, connecticut
ulrich franzen
1956–58

Nine inverted steel umbrellas compose the vault of this dramatic glass-walled house. They immediately inspired a cartoon by Alan Dunn, in which the owner explains to a friend: "All I asked was a roof over my head and, dammit, that's what I got!" In fact, Henry and Shavan Towers got far more: a powerful yet graceful 3,000-square-foot pavilion frames a spectacular view over the Connecticut River estuary and a wide sweep of protected wetlands. And a stone-walled podium of bedrooms, solidly rooted in the hillside, accomodated the Towers and the three children they raised here. The masonry leads the eye to natural rock outcrops; the glass is a wonderful mix of reflection and transparency.

The Towers were inspired to build it after spending weekends at a Breuer house Shavan's parents had built in Williamstown in 1947. "It was only 36 by 48 feet, but it felt liberating after our Federal house in Essex," recalls Mr. Towers. "We bought this 75-acre site and, after looking at the work of fifteen architects, picked Franzen—because he was our age, a student of Breuer, and had built a house for himself with his own money—a good test of his ideas and practicality. He asked us for a wish list and spent several weekends up here—but it was always foggy, so he had to take our word for the view."

Franzen was born in Germany, worked for I.M. Pei after getting his master's degree at Harvard, and admits that "the most important influence in my life was Mies." He has designed about 65 houses, in addition to many large buildings, but this

Above Wide eaves shade the glass walls and frame a panoramic view over the Essex River.

Opposite A stone-walled podium of bedrooms is rooted in the hillside below the pavilion that encloses the living areas.

Overleaf The steel frame with its slender columns and channels was built in a local shipyard and erected in a day.

LOWER LEVEL   MAIN LEVEL

early example remains one of his favorites. The steel frame, with its slender columns and channels marking the 20-by-20-foot grid was built in a local shipyard and erected in a day. A canopy of stained cypress boards shades the wide deck and glass (thermopane below and plate above), which is set into handsomely detailed mullions. The upstairs floor is oak block; the downstairs cork on concrete. "The craft heritage was still alive when we built this house," the owners recall, "and it was put together like a boat, with every joint exposed."

Within the soaring, open-plan interior, the galley kitchen is enclosed by white cabinets, which also separate the staircase, dining, and breakfast areas from the living room that occupies the south half of the space. Only the black chimney and kitchen flue link floor and vault, and thus the entire upper floor is considered, for tax purposes, a single room.

Few changes have been made in 43 years. The owners still cherish the craft rocker and the Aalto, Knoll, and Danish modern furniture they bought when they moved in. A wall of the stair hall has been covered with mirror glass to create the illusion of space. One of the Towers' daughters became an architect and has added a walled pool that complements the art works placed around the house.

Opposite The Towers cherish the classic modern furniture they bought when they moved in.

Above The dining area has an intimacy that contrasts with the expansive living room.

Top A view of the vaulted ceiling that rises above the stair hall.

miller house

columbus, indiana
eero saarinen
1957–58
interiors by alexander girard

J. Irwin Miller is a Medici of modern architecture, who used his position as chairman of the Cummins Engine Company to sponsor nearly 70 public buildings in his home town of Columbus, Indiana. In 1957, he established a foundation that pays the fees of notable architects selected from an approved list. Six of their buildings have been named National Historic Landmarks—a first for modernism and an extraordinary achievement for a small midwestern

town. One of them is the house that Miller and his wife, Xenia, commissioned from their friend Eero Saarinen, who had earlier built them a summer house they still use on Lake Rousseau in Ontario.

Saarinen brought Dan Kiley to landscape the eleven acres of farmland and Alexander Girard, a master of color and pattern, to design the interiors. They collaborated to achieve an ideal integration of nature, structure, and furnishings. As precisely tooled as one of the Cummins engines, the house is a work of art in which slate cladding, interior walls of white marble, broad windows, and travertine floors are contained within a structural frame of slender steel columns. These support a roof deck that

is slightly inclined to shed rain and pierced by linear skylights. The skylights follow the grid of the columns and provide a soft, even illumination throughout the house and beneath the shady eaves. Five children were raised here—William Miller is continuing his father's work as an architecture patron—yet the original furnishings have survived in pristine condition, and the house has a timeless serenity.

The house was the product of a creative dialogue. "Eero proposed different schemes and we said 'go back and try again,' since we didn't want to tell him what to do," recalls Mrs. Miller. "His first design was raised on stilts in the woods among the mosquitoes. I turned that down right away!" Later she told him,

"I don't want to live in the same house for the rest of my life— what are you going to do about that?" He replied: "I'm going to build a neutral structure and all the color is going into the drapes and furnishings. Any time you want a new house you can throw them away and start all over again!"

Ceilings are high to provide good acoustics for music making; however, Girard proposed one of the first conversation pits to eliminate the clutter of seating in the expansive living room. The cushions are changed, twice a year, from cream to red and back to mark the passage of the seasons. Saarinen offered some of his first pedestal dining chairs as an alternative to the Eames's forest of legs.

Opposite The terrace is protected by the cantilevered roof plane and is used for much of the year as an outdoor room.

Above Dan Kiley landscaped the 11-acre estate, planting an allee of trees that frame a Henry Moore bronze.

Overleaf Slate cladding sets off the slender white columns and travertine pavers.

FIRST FLOOR

136

Built-in bookshelves, major art works, and Girard's boldly patterned rugs stand out with startling clarity. One rug incorporates the family's initials, a "Y" for Yale, a "C" for Cummins, and favorite symbols. There is a tiny fountain, with live orchids and whimsical ceramic figures by Girard's brother, Tunsi, at the center of the round, marble-topped Saarinen table. Yet, even here, beauty is tempered by practicality. "We have five children and we're messy eaters," Miller told the designer. "Why don't you incorporate food spots into the rug?"

The house is raised above the flood level of the river, and Kiley has created outdoor rooms, as well as an allee of trees with a Lipschitz at one end and a Moore at the other, which provides welcome shade on summer days. The Millers have taken down one interior wall to enlarge a guest room, but their fear that they would "rattle around" when their children were grown was misplaced; they still use every part of the house and garden.

Above An early example of the conversation pit, devised by Girard to eliminate the clutter of seating

Top A fountain and ceramic figures by Tunsi Girard make a centerpiece for the Saarinen pedestal table.

Opposite, top Built-in bookshelves line one wall of the living room, echoing the crisp geometry of the structural grid.

Opposite Alexander Girard's colorful rugs and fabrics complement the white marble walls and travertine floor.

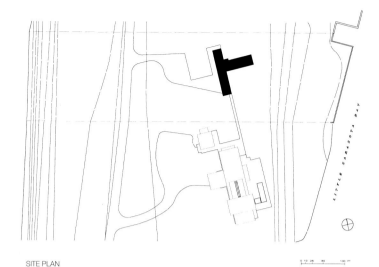

burkhardt house

casey key, florida
paul rudolph
1956–57
restored 1991; guest house,
toshiko mori, 1999

Paul Rudolph was the star of the Sarasota School of postwar modern architecture, opening his office in that city in 1952, and designing houses and schools that became increasingly monumental in scale and complexity through the end of the decade. They anticipated the dizzying triplex he built for himself in New York, the daring cantilevers of the Bass house in Fort Worth, and the massive Yale School of Art and Architecture. Even the grandest of these early

houses has a taut elegance and is perfectly suited to the subtropical climate. A few—such as the Walker guest house on Sanibel Island—are still imperiled, but others have been rescued, notably the Umbrella House on Lido Shores, which Gary and Carol Stover have restored to its original condition (except for its trademark pergola).

Burkhardt was a German businessman who wintered here with his family until 1973, but this 4,000-square-foot house could be lived in year-round. Located on a narrow barrier island, it is a linear post-and-beam structure with concrete block walls. It is set back behind a graveled yard and opens up to the east over a pool terrace and shady lawn to the intercoastal

waterway. Cantilevered roof planes shade the main floor and the upstairs office, and a broad jutting canopy protects the entrance. Deep joists diffuse light entering from the lantern over the double-height living room, which was originally a screened breezeway. The original guest house/garage stands off to the north.

Betsey Cohen, a Philadelphia banker, and her husband Edward, a classical historian, bought the house in 1981 for its simple lines and placement on the site. Cohen wept when she saw how it had been brutalized by its second owner. It made sense to glaze the central section and install air conditioning, but the skylight and the rear of the house had been blocked off.

A barbecue occupied the former conversation pit, the cream terrazzo floor was covered in pink shag rug, and there was a wildly inappropriate kidney-shaped pool in back. The Cohens unblocked the windows, replaced the roof membrane, removed the carpet and cleaned up, but spent ten winters in the house before undertaking a major upgrade.

Drawing on her experience from adaptive reuse projects in Philadelphia, Mrs. Cohen supervised the installation of a new pool, low-voltage lighting, and cabinetry that enhances the exposed concrete-block walls, and a sliding screen of etched glass to enclose the dining room. Classic modern furniture and artworks seem to hover in

Opposite A sliding screen of etched glass was added to separate the dining room from the living room.

Overleaf Cantilvered roof planes shade the house and add drama to the upstairs office.

the subtly gradated light that filters down from the skylight and the clerestories on each side of the dining room. The master bedroom is a tranquil retreat, with a bed set on a concrete block platform and the sunlight diffused by folded paper blinds. Stairs lead up to a small office with a sweeping view.

Toshiko Mori was commissioned to design a 3,000-square-foot guesthouse for the Cohens' three grown children on the footprint of a neighboring house that was destroyed by a hurricane. Powerful and crisply detailed, it is raised above the flood level on concrete pilotis and divided into two narrow bars—a bedroom suite, living room, and terrace to the west and a duplex of bedroom suites to east, linked by open steel steps—to reduce its bulk. Mori lined up the longer bar on a path leading from the pool terrace to establish a connection between the two houses, and selected a similar concrete block for the walls. However, she raised the pilotis a foot more than the regulations required to place the rooms within the tree canopy. As she explains, "Rudolph's house is horizontal, mine is vertical; his is a tree trunk, rooted in the ground; mine is like a tree top."

Opposite A roof lantern and clerestories balance the light in the central living room.

Above Spare furnishings and exposed concrete blocks make the master bedroom a cool retreat.

Top Toshiko Mori's L-plan guest house is lofted on pilotis and complements the house.

deering house

casey key, florida
paul rudolph
1959–60
restored 1999–2000

The culmination of Rudolph's work in Sarasota was this nobly proportioned, 4,350-square-foot villa, which was built for the Deerings, a mature couple with grown children, to enjoy year-round. A temple-like structure of hard lime-concrete blocks, it is raised a few feet above the dunes of the Gulf Coast and has defied a succession of storms. The concrete picks up on the tone of the sand and is coated with silicon to repel moisture. The majestic rhythm of the columns, faced with painted cypress, is softened on the east side by gridded wood screens. These are reprised along the bedroom corridor and admit breezes while filtering the harsh sunlight, much like the grilles in Islamic architecture. On the west side, the columns frame a two-story loggia with a cream terrazzo floor. It opens up to the ocean through removable glass-fiber mesh screens. Rooms on four levels are enclosed by glass sliders and open onto this heroically scaled porch, which is at once indoors and outdoors. The kitchen and intimate dining room open directly off the loggia; the living room steps up from the north end; and the master suite, a guest bedroom, and a mezzanine-level bridge look down into it.

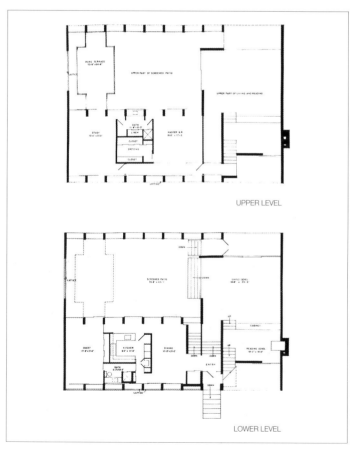

UPPER LEVEL

LOWER LEVEL

Top Palms screen the garden façade of the house with its gridded wooden screens.

Opposite Detail of beach façade: a temple-like structure of hard lime-concrete blocks

Above A mezzanine gallery overlooks the two-story loggia, which can be enclosed with mesh screens.

Opposite Massive glass sliders enclose the living room, which is raised a few feet above the loggia.

149

Neglected by subsequent owners, the house was extensively refurbished by M & M Homes of Sarasota, which replaced the sagging steel roof beam and the rotting wood facing of the columns on the Gulf side. The sun screens were cleaned, the terrazzo floors were patched and reground, and tempered glass replaced the original. Ductwork was upgraded, the cypress kitchen cabinets were stripped, and the concrete block was cleaned. Other improvements were less felicitous: propping up the cantilevered treads of the entry stairs with concrete blocks, substituting granite for the stainless steel counter tops, and introducing incongruous new light fittings—but these shortcomings can easily be remedied. The builders wisely had second thoughts about excavating the loggia to accommodate a pool and spa. At the time of writing, this unique house awaits an owner who will give the restoration a final polish.

Opposite Steps leading from the two-level living area with its built-in storage and stereo cabinets

Above The concrete blocks pick up on the color of the sand and are coated with silicon to repel moisture.

Top Sliding wood grids enclose the bedrooms, evoking the fretted screens of Islamic architecture.

esherick house

philadelphia, pennsylvania
louis kahn
1959–61

In the buildings of Louis I. Kahn one discovers the heroic vision and anguished execution of a Michelangelo, and a similar appeal to an inner truth. "Architecture is a thoughtful making of spaces," he observed. "It is not filling prescriptions as clients want them filled." The Kimbell Art Museum in Fort Worth, the Salk Institute in La Jolla, and a dozen other masterworks validate his uncompromising stance, but he found few residential clients. One of those few

was Margaret Esherick, though the commission came from her father, Wharton, and she never moved in. A Christian Scientist, she died of untreated pneumonia soon after the 2,300-square-foot house was completed. The second owners were unaware of its importance, and it stood empty for two years until, in 1981, Robert and Lynn Gallagher bought and restored it. The house that Vincent Scully called "a chalice of light" finally found the custodians it deserved.

The Gallaghers sought expert advice and skilled craftspeople before embarking on a year-long restoration. Water had warped the apitong floor boards, and huge sheets of glass were sagging—which required the insertion of a steel beam. It took

six months to find the right tone of sand for the concrete stucco. "The house is a work of art and we wanted to keep it pure," says Ms. Gallagher, a marketing consultant. Her husband is a dentist whose sense of perfectionism was sharpened by restoring classic cars. "We kept asking,

'what would Kahn have done,' and then discovered that everyone who worked for him went broke because he made so many changes."

The couple's persistence was amply rewarded. One can now enjoy not only the rude grandeur of the concrete shell

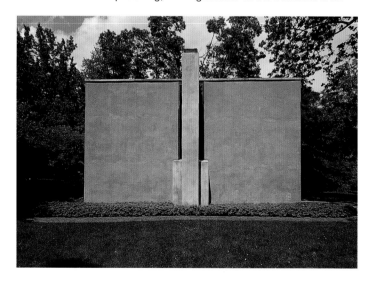

Above A chimney bisecting a tall window in the blank west side gives the house a monumental quality.

Opposite The abstract geometry of the garden façade is enhanced by the bold modeling of wood and concrete.

KITCHEN

LAUNDRY

DINING ROOM

LIVING ROOM

FOYER

0 5   15

FIRST FLOOR

153

and distinctive geometry of each wall, but also the subtle interplay of tones and textures, horizontal and vertical thrusts. Kahn made inventive use of a T-motif in the openings on each facade. Windows are precisely placed to frame treetops and a freestanding chimney; they alternate with wooden flaps that open to provide cross ventilation. Margaret Esherick was a bookseller, and a wall of shelves play off the ivory stucco walls. Her father Wharton, a craftsman, designed the kitchen cabinets, copper sink, and stair rail. A massive wood stair and gallery divide the soaring living room from the dining room and kitchen below, and the master suite above, each volume a subdivision of another. The bedroom extends from front to back and is flanked by a screened bathing/dressing area with a sunken tub, shower, and closet shoehorned into a narrow space.

In this house, the architect showed that, while professing to value the abstract above the pragmatic, he could prescribe just what his clients needed.

Opposite A balcony outside the upstairs bedroom overlooks the double-height living room.

Above Kahn made inventive use of a "T" motif, especially here in the entrance façade.

Top The house from the street, its austere cubic form softened by luxuriant plantings

one architect, three strategies

Through his 45 years of practice in southern California, the Austrian emigré Richard Neutra created more than 180 houses and apartment buildings, and most were variations on a simple theme: a handsomely proportioned white stucco box with ribbon windows that opened up to nature. Stone and brick were used where appropriate, but he preferred to set off his white planes with metal trim (or aluminum-painted wood) to create what he called "a machine in the garden." Neutra's genius was to adapt International Style minimalism to the benign climate and casual lifestyle of southern California, and his rigorous geometry in combination with an indoors-outdoors flow of space has made these houses immensely appealing to a new generation of owners. Here are three, from successive decades, which have been inventively extended, restored, or reinterpreted.

lewin house

santa monica, california
richard neutra
1938
restored and extended by
steven ehrlich, 1998

Sandwiched between palm-fringed palisades and gleaming sand is this sleek, white beach house, which was built for Albert Lewin—the producer of such classic movies as *Mutiny on the Bounty* and *The Good Earth*, a literate writer-director, and an enthusiastic collector of modern art. Max Ernst, Man Ray, and Jean Renoir were among his dinner guests; following Lewin, Mae West lived here. Gwathmey Siegel added a pool surrounded with Mexican tiles; a black granite hearth and bookshelves; dark gray, brown, and green walls. When the present owners bought the 5,800-square-foot house in 1988, they resolved to restore its integrity, but deferred major work until they were able to acquire the neighboring lot. To direct the restoration and add space for entertaining, a guest suite, larger staff quarters, and parking, they selected Steven Ehrlich, who had launched his practice in 1981 with a studio in the garden of a Neutra house in the Hollywood Hills.

Here, the challenge was to create a much larger addition that would flow out of the taut glass and stucco original, while respecting its materials and proportions. The architect and project director Jim Schmidt extruded a guest bedroom over a rebuilt garage, achieving a seamless join with the original structure. He also extended the housekeeper's apartment over a second double garage with brushed stainless doors, creating an impassive new façade of white stucco and poured concrete that helps exclude the roar of traffic from the busy coast highway.

Behind this addition, floating like an ark in a sea of grass, is a pavilion with a stainless-steel cycloidal vault, perforated on the underside to absorb sound, which was inspired by the similar roofs of Louis Kahn's Kimbell Art Museum. It subtly echoes the rounded glass bay of the house, to which it is linked by a glass walkway. As a way to dematerialize this massive structure, it is supported on slender steel outrigger columns on the side nearest the house, and the glass walls at either end can be fully retracted to open the interior to ocean breezes. The inner side is also of glass; to the south, poured concrete walls define the boundary of the site and enclose a kitchen-buffet and a bathroom. The concrete floor was acid-washed to achieve varied textures.

Ehrlich has used the new structure to enhance the old and to siphon off the boisterous activities of the beach and the owners' small son. A strong axis flows from a grassy court through the pavilion and a new pool to a motorized gate in the garden wall. This glides open to

Above Looking down from the Santa Monica Palisades onto the extended house

Opposite A curved bay enclosing the living room, which projects out towards the ocean

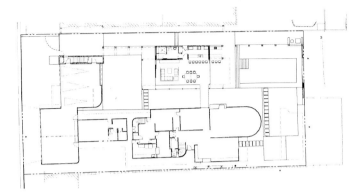

FIRST FLOOR

159

reveal the beach and to frame a lifeguard station. The brushed stainless steel and concrete have greater density than the silver-trimmed stucco, but employ the same restrained palette. "I've drawn on sixty years of technology to make Neutra's dream come true and to achieve a balance of the serene and the kinetic," says the architect.

The interior of the old house has been scrupulously restored by the wife, with advice from Tom Callaway, and enhanced by period light sconces and other fittings. The wood floor was sanded and bleached, and new aluminum-trimmed Vitrolite bathrooms replicate those that survived unchanged. The awnings that shade the south side of the house were remade.

Gwathmey's colors are gone (along with his tiled pool) and the luminous white rooms are furnished with modern pieces by Robsjohn-Gibbings and Jean Prouve, along with museum-quality aluminum-framed chairs, chaises, and tables by Warren McArthur, Neutra's contemporary. In the pavilion, his high stools are drawn up to the bar, and one of his armchairs joins other seating on a gray rug, giving this indoor-outdoor space an air of quiet sophistication.

Opposite A massive concrete wall and slender steel columns support cycloidal steel vault of the new garden pavilion.

Above Outrigger columns and wild grass bridge the gap between the pavilion and the house with its retractable awnings.

Top The cycloidal vault was inspired by Louis Kahn's Kimball Art Museum and plays off the curved bay of the house.

Opposite The wood floor was sanded and bleached as part of a comprehensive restoration.

Above Furniture by Warren MacArthur, Jean Prouve, and Robbsjohn-Gibbings enhance the period flavor.

kaufmann house

palm springs, california
richard neutra
1946–47
restored by marmol & radziner
1993–97

Edgar Kaufmann, a Pittsburgh department store magnate, commissioned Fallingwater as a summer house, and, a decade later, this 3,200-square-foot winter retreat. Each is a masterpiece and has become legendary—chiefly through iconic photos. The Wright, however, was always cherished, whereas the Neutra was mutilated and might easily have been torn down. In 1991, it was bought by a dedicated couple, Brent and Beth Harris, who supervised an exemplary restoration and are now recreating the landscape that was integral to Neutra's concept.

The Harrises—he is a marketing executive, she an architectural historian—were searching for a classic modern house and found this tattered treasure, which had been on the market for a long time. Five successive owners had pushed out walls, enclosed a patio, and loaded the roof with service ducts. The interior was wallpapered, carpeted, and cluttered with Louis-something furniture. Pseudo-Spanish tract houses were advancing from every side, blocking views of desert and mountains. "Another owner might have razed or remodeled it, but that didn't feel right to

Above Stone, wood, and concrete flow through the glass entry door.

Opposite Aluminum louvers on the rooftop gloriette contrast with the desert landscape.

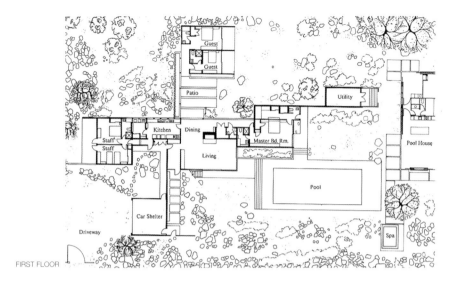

FIRST FLOOR

166

us," says Brent. As they spent more time in the house, conducted intensive archival research, and looked at the 60 photos Julius Shulman had taken in the late 1940s, they realized that removing additions would not be enough. "We gradually discovered how rich it was and decided, since it wasn't our principal home, to treat it as a work of art," explains Beth.

They developed a comprehensive plan to deal with the house as a whole and take it back to its original condition, drawing on the expertise of Shulman, architectural historian David Gebhardt, and Albert Frey—a longtime resident of Palm Springs who built a neighboring house for designer Raymond Loewy in the same year

the Kaufmann house was built. "Red" Marsh, a contractor who built a score of Neutra houses and was now in his eighties, offered advice. To realize their vision, the Harrises chose Marmol and Radziner, a design-build firm in Los Angeles that had already become a leader in the restoration of mid-century modern houses, as well as in new construction. Over the next five years, architects and clients discussed every issue and detail, insisting that the materials and techniques be as authentic as possible. In what Leo Marmol called "an archeological dig," layers of additions were stripped to discover if original materials had survived and could be refurbished. To replicate missing elements, a quarry was reopened

to secure the right tone of Utah sandstone. Sources were located around the country for mica to bring a sparkle to the plaster and for crimped sheet metal to fill missing sections of the fascia.

The challenge of working through the hot summer and locating elusive items prolonged the project two years beyond schedule, but the Harrises refused to compromise. "With our love of architecture, how could we have walked away?" asks Brent, rhetorically. "It was agonizing at times but it also gave us one of the most fulfilling experiences of our lives." They learned that Kaufmann was equally involved, exchanging daily letters with Neutra over a period of nine months. "We were

Previous spread Crisp cubes of glass and stucco anchored by flanking stone walls

Opposite From the gloriette you can forget encroaching suburbia and bask in the warm desert wind

Above During the five-year restoration, the house was stripped to its structural core and every element was refurbished or replaced.

168

interested in finding out how it was built, not just how it looked," says Beth. "They told us no one would know the difference if they put a thin layer of plaster over board on the living room wall, rather than building it up as a solid one-and-a-half-inch mass. But *we* would know, and shortcuts can always be sensed by the way a room sounds or holds heat." Everything was exactly reproduced, from the Fresnel lenses in the ceiling lights to the patterns of grain in the douglas fir soffits and birch ply cabinets. Bold colors, cork cladding, and T-section door handles were all restored.

The one essential improvement was to integrate the air conditioning that had been crudely superimposed—to make the house habitable year-round and to protect it from drying out in the furnace heat of summer. The architects spent months pressing the mechanical engineer to design thinner ducts, threading them in below the radiant heating elements in areas where damaged concrete had to be replaced and up through walls as these were being seismically upgraded. Vents were concealed in cabinets and under beds.

Another important addition is Marmol and Radziner's new pool house, which replaces an unsightly structure, conceals the tennis court, and contains features the Kaufmanns never envisaged—including a media room and play space for two small children, a gym, a steam

Above Patterns of wood grain, colors of stone, and light fittings were precisely matched to vintage photographs.

Opposite, top The sparely furnished master bedroom opens up to the terrace and can be screened off by translucent drapes.

Opposite A view of the new pool house, designed by Marmol and Radziner

171

shower, and complex mechanical and security controls. It respects Neutra's scale without mimicking his style, and its sliding glass windows and chalky green walls allow it to fade into the background. A close-cropped lawn extends like a carpet from house to pool, and then the desert takes over. Native trees screen an enlarged boundary, blocking off red tile roofs, and the boulders and cacti lead the eye to the vista of mountains.

Once again, the house has a magical presence, its crisp cubes of glass and stucco anchored by flanking stone walls reaching out into the wilderness. At sunset, a warm wind often blows down the valley, drowning the chatter of cicadas and rattling the aluminum louvers that shelter the patio and rooftop gloriette. Within, every room is precisely composed, every object thoughtfully chosen. Mirrors draw the landscape inside, the roof plane leads the eye out. The Harrises see the house as a piece of sculpture that shapes their perceptions, and as a place to live—simply and in a state of tranquillity.

Opposite Eames chairs that are contemporary with the house sit on a Raymond Loewy rug.

Above New appliances complement original ovens and cork surfaces in the galley kitchen.

Top The living room opens up on two sides through sliding glass windows.

levinsohn house

bel air, california
richard neutra
1955–56
restored by lorcan o'herlihy
1999–2001

Good movies, like good buildings, are the product of personal vision and collaborative effort, of strategy and attention to detail. So it is no surprise that Gary Levinsohn, an executive producer of *Saving Private Ryan* and *The Patriot*, should spend as much time and effort in getting his house to come out right as he does in putting something memorable on the screen. As soon as finances allowed, his wife Pia, a graduate student of psychology, went looking for a

modern classic. "When she saw this, she knew she'd found the right thing, even though they had shortened the skirt and added lipstick to sell it," he explains. "The owner believed he had something special and someone with more money tried to outbid us. But we wrote him a letter persuading him to sell to us, and ended up completely hooked."

It is a house with a strong linear axis, set up on a hillside, with a master suite and living areas raised a story above the garage, maid's quarters, and service rooms. Stucco walls frame an exterior staircase that was later enclosed with steel-framed glass. A shed roof with exposed joists tilts down to shade south-facing areas and to

admit light and views of tree tops through the north-facing clerestory. The house was one of ten that Neutra designed in 1955, and whatever he may have done to shape the interior had been changed by later owners. But the proportions were handsome and each space flowed easily into the next. The challenge was to remove accretions, to

enhance the sense of openness, and to push the house to a higher level of excellence.

The Levinsohns already had their architect, Lorcan O'Herlihy, a committed modernist who apprenticed with I. M. Pei and Steven Holl and who had earlier upgraded their 1970s house in a nearby canyon. "I've always been interested in doing a fresh

Above A hillside house with the master suite and living areas raised a story above the garage and services

Opposite A shed roof with exposed joists slopes down to shelter the south façade; stucco walls enclose the entrance staircase.

take on the modern movement, and this felt like a springboard," he says. "We respected, but didn't feel constrained by, what we found." The owners wanted to be fully involved and to live in the house while it was being improved, which required that work be done in stages, one area at a time.

Walls and soffits were replaced to make the interior seamless; a new maple floor was installed, and the stair hall and entry area were paved with limestone. A gym occupies what was once a small patio and is concealed behind a folding screen of wood-framed translucent glass. A bathroom was turned into a dressing area, and a bedroom closet was removed to open up a view down a

passage and across the open living room—almost the full length of the 2,800-square-foot upper level. At the far end, tucked in behind a massive hearth of Texas fossil stone, is an intimate media room with two day beds and artfully concealed equipment. The downstairs wine cellar was rebuilt, and open space was enclosed to provide a music studio and an office.

O'Herlihy sketched intricate cabinets and restrained furniture that would be custom-made in maple and cherry, reviewing his designs with the owners, who contributed their own suggestions. Everything was precisely crafted and aligned to preserve the horizontality of the space and not interrupt its flow. Elliptical louvers of maple backed with

Above A strong linear axis links a succession of spaces that open into each other.

Top The breakfast area is lit from a circular skylight, and louvers can be rotated to shut off the kitchen

Opposite Lorcan O'Herlihy designed blocky maple and leather seating to define the living area.

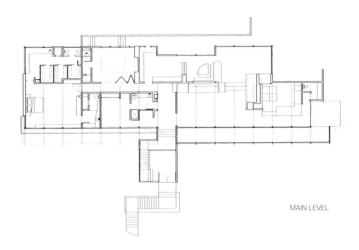

MAIN LEVEL

aluminum can be rotated to screen off the kitchen from the raised dining area. A long-tapered coffee table of sand-blasted glass on a Carlo Scarpa steel base is flanked by leather-cushioned chairs and a sofa. The art was chosen with equal care. A Roy Lichtenstein silkscreen print of an interior fills an entire wall of the master bed-room; the owners' greatest enthusiasm, however, is for clas-sic black and white photo-graphs. The simple frames by the S. K. Josephsburg Studio are so perfectly crafted that small images command large spaces.

Expanses of black granite, inserted by a former owner in the living room, will be replaced with limestone and split-face buff sandstone to transform a dark void into a floating volume, and the same sandstone will clad the walls of the stair hall, which will be given a new steel and glass balustrade. "This house has no secrets," says Levinsohn. "The internal divi-sions are cut away and the expansive windows bring the outside in. However, as with music, the simpler it is, the more lies behind it." As O'Herlihy and he continue the process of refinement, the house realizes the potential it always had, but never before achieved.

Opposite One wall in the master bed-room is covered with a silkscreen print by Roy Lichtenstein

Above View from the bedroom past the folding glass doors that enclose the gym

Top An open hearth separates the raised dining area from an intimate media room.

more second acts

Before and after World War II, progressive architects took pride in designing minimum shelter at modest expense, posing a challenge to new owners who seek to enhance or to extend these frugal spaces while respecting their original character. Even affluent clients were frustrated when their architect's vision outran budgets or available technology, but some of these houses have since been upgraded and given a new life.

yates house

silver lake, california
r.m. schindler
1938 , 47
restored by amy murphy
1996 – 99

R. M. Schindler was born in Vienna, came to America to work with Wright, and built a succession of influential houses during his 30-year practice in Los Angeles. In contrast to Neutra, a former classmate who quickly achieved fame, Schindler was a fiercely independent spirit who created miracles of spatial invention on miniscule budgets. Even his smallest jobs—such as the performance space he designed for music critic Peter Yates and his concert pianist wife, Frances Mullen—were touched by genius. The couple lived with their three small children and his grandmother in a 900-square-foot bungalow, but they valued art over creature comforts and scraped together $2,700 to build a pitch-vaulted upstairs room seating 50, where Mullen and her friends could perform avant-garde music. These "Concerts on the Roof" featured premieres by John Cage, Arnold Schoenberg, and other emigrés, and gave birth to a celebrated series at the Los Angeles County Museum of Art.

Schindler also remodeled the façade of the bungalow, creating a collage of white stucco and brown asphalt shingles to complement the original clapboards.

He inserted a stair over the entry, but left the downstairs rooms unchanged; a decade later he added an upstairs master bedroom. Thomas Anderson, an experimental filmmaker and Cal Arts professor, bought the house in 1996 for its potential—even though it was sagging, overgrown, and had been crudely divided into two rental units. The original stair was blocked off by closets, there was extensive water damage, and the foundation had settled. One of his students recommended architectural designer Amy Murphy for restoration, and what began as a structural upgrade blossomed into a meticulous restoration of Schindler's original, working from two plates of his drawings.

Murphy stabilized the house on caissons, matched original color samples, and added redwood fins to the roof as the architect had intended. Schindler's spirit also infuses the first floor, which Murphy stripped to its studs, substituting a complex of open spaces for the warren of little rooms.

"Until we got into construction we didn't know what we could save," explains Murphy. "We made discoveries about the house, and what Schindler's intentions were. Downstairs, I had to make judgment calls— what to cut, how far to try to match the original materials. A windowless, nine-foot wide passage at the center became a dining alcove and part of a diagonal axis through the entire

Opposite Schindler added an upper story to a modest wood bungalow, creating a collage of shapes and materials.

183

space, with a wood post (added to reinforce the structure) as anchor. I was interested in the abstract typology of modern space, transparent and overlapping."

Low bookcases defining the entry, built-in shelves, and the stair are stained the original olive green to contrast with the sharp white geometry of the walls and a new floor of douglas fir. In the music room, light shimmers off the grain of olive-stained plywood on the walls and the asymmetrical pitched vault. Windows command an ocean view and open onto a broad, asphalt-boarded deck with a pipe-rail balustrade and projecting pergola on two sides. Contemporary and classic modern furniture enrich the interior. Carlo Scarpa's massive plywood

dining table and leather side chairs complement the spare, angular armchairs by Umberto Riva, and upstairs the Vladimir Kagan desk chair and Robert Nicolais's replicas of two Schindler chairs from the Kings Road house. Anderson, who shares the house with his wife, Sung Tae Kim, feels he is perpetuating an artistic tradition.

Opposite Following a structural upgrade, Murphy opened up and remodeled the unimproved ground floor.

Above Adventurous new music was performed in this vaulted room launching a celebrated avant-garde series.

Top A white stucco wall encloses the front yard, blocking off the original bungalow.

MAIN FLOOR

RESIDENCE R ROTH
LOS ANGELES CALIFORNIA 1946
R.M. SCHINDLER, ARCH.

GROUND FLOOR

roth house

studio city, california
r.m. schindler
1945–46
restored 1999

Dramatically perched on the edge of a steep hill, this is a house of parts that seem to be in motion, constantly rearranging themselves into new and provocative compositions. One approaches from around the curved gray stucco wall of a garage (entered from either end, but too narrow for contemporary cars) and a turf-covered deck that is propped above it on narrow wood struts. At street level, the house appears as a simple rectalinear box, with few

inflections, but from above it resembles an angular mono-chromatic sculpture: an assemblage of square and triangle, wedge and cube, all topped with white gravel. It's set in a pastoral landscape of gardens and foothills that conceal the commercial-suburban sprawl of the San Fernando Valley, with a distant view of mountains on a clear day.

Nothing seems to have changed in the half-century since it was built, but two years ago it was in terrible condition and was sold to Noam and Jasmyne Murro as a tear-down. Noam grew up in a Bauhaus residence in Jerusalem and studied architecture before becoming a director of commercials; his wife programs the Los Angeles Independent Film Festival.

"When we moved to L.A. we wanted to find a great modern house and this was the first we saw," he recalls. "It would be nice if it were 50 percent larger, but we were after quality, not quantity. It has soul, honesty, and playfulness and it's timeless. The longer you live in a Schindler, the more you appreciate his brilliance."

Before moving in at the end of 1999, they undertook a major restoration with help from contractor Jeff Fink, replacing the roof together with many of the windows, which had rotted where the sun had caught them. They installed air conditioning and some additional Schindler-like glass light boxes in the low ceilings. A big hall closet was

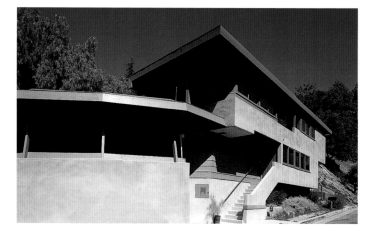

Above A turf-covered deck is propped above the curved garage; steps lead up to the two levels of the house.

Opposite An expansive window frames a view to the west of the Hollywood Hills.

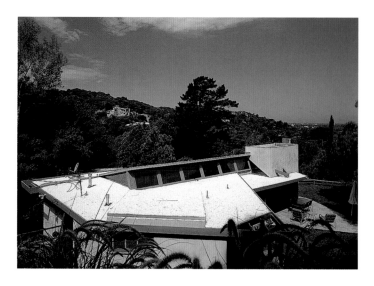

186

sliced in half to provide added storage in the kitchen, which was upgraded in the spirit of the original, using vertical wood pulls rather than hardware on the new Douglas fir cabinets. The walls had been repeatedly overpainted, so the Murros changed the interior stucco from green to white, and the exterior walls to pale gray with a darker gray for the joinery, adding a board to the roof fascia to conceal wiring for industrial light fittings.

Now everyone can appreciate what the Murros saw from the start. In the long living room, one's eye is drawn along by a tilted clerestory, sending light shimmering over the ribbed surface of the shallow pitched vault of green-stained redwood and the plywood below. It casts a

bar of light along the polished redwood floor and the ramp that substitutes for steps at the rear. Light from side windows and the west bay is modulated by wood Venetian blinds. Glass set into the angle of the vault illuminates intricate shifts of joists and the juxtaposition of plain and textured wood. Opening off this linear space is the kitchen and a hexagonal glass-walled breakfast room. In back is the master bedroom, which looks into the living room though a wall of glass protected by folding wooden shutters, and a guest bedroom that is rotated off the trunk of the house at a 45-degree angle. Glenn Murcutt, Australia's best architect, paid a visit, thought this the best Schindler he had seen, and shot 30 reels of film.

Above Schindler's mastery of detail is evident in the stone hearth and intricate geometry of the wood-frame structure.

Top This view from the upper garden shows how the guest room juts from the linear house.

Opposite A tilted clerestory sends light shimmering over the ribbed surface of the shallow-pitched ceiling vault.

dubin-cheselka house

mar vista, california
ain, johnson, & day
1946–49
restored by david hertz/
syndesis, 1997–99

Huge shade trees tower over tiny cubic houses with flat roofs extending out to unfenced front yards on three parallel streets. Together, they form an idyllic, tight-knit community that has been carefully maintained and sensitively enhanced. Conceived as an enlightened speculative development that would bring good design to the masses, the principal architect of this project was Gregory Ain, a social activist who apprenticed with Neutra and opened his L. A. office in 1935.

Ain's houses were always plain and practical, and every one of the 1,050 square feet in these affordable homes was intensively used. Movable walls turned one bedroom into a pair or would fold back to unite living room and den. The pass-though counter from the kitchen could seat six or serve as a buffet bar. Expansive windows, shaded by a projecting canopy, opened onto a rear patio that served as an outdoor room. The houses sold for about $13,000, which was well above average at that time, and the strongest appeal was to architects, academics, and engineers at the nearby Douglas Aircraft plant.

Prices now range up to $650,000, but the young professionals who are reinvigorating this West Los Angeles neighborhood still find it a great place to bring up kids, socialize with neighbors, and enjoy Ain's spare yet elastic spaces. That's the reaction of Mitch Dubin, a camera operator, and his artist wife, Kim Cheselka. "We had a clean open loft in New York, and didn't want a cottage with boxy little rooms," she says. "This was in funky condition but the bones were good. We worked like maniacs for a few months, stripping away cheap ply, shag rug, asbestos ceiling tile, and a

Above Hertz added an angled pergola to Ain's plain, practical cottage.

Opposite The shaded deck overlooks the pool and serves as an outdoor room.

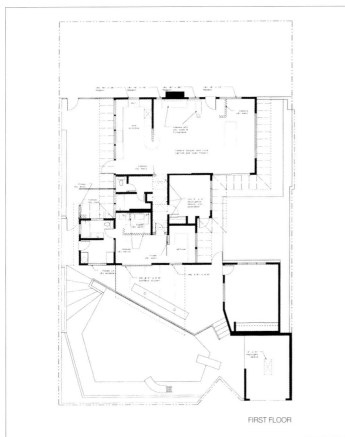

FIRST FLOOR

walk-in closet that blocked the light in the 350-square-foot addition to the rear. David is a big fan of Ain, so we asked him to take it back to what it was."

The sliding walls that were an important feature of the original design had been removed and were not replaced. Hertz took out another wall and opened the kitchen up to the living room, substituting a laminated ply disc for the pass through. To wash the center of the house with light, he added and enlarged windows and skylights. A side window frames a bamboo-screened courtyard, and the master bedroom opens onto a new redwood deck through a sliding glass barn door, with a tiny window placed high in one corner for a glimpse

of tree tops. The furniture is a mix of vintage modern and contemporary craft.

"We live minimally, so stripping away and opening up was the obvious course, pulling in light and breezes, with perimeter walls to ensure privacy," says Dubin. "Then we waited eighteen months to catch our breath and enjoy the experience of living here before upgrading the exterior. We sandblasted the spray-on coating and replaced it with integrally colored stucco in as dark an olive green as we could get, and added a redwood pergola over the deck. The studio-garage will be rebuilt in phase three."

Opposite A circular breakfast table links the kitchen to the expansive living-dining area.

Above Walls were removed to create an open plan, within which a sitting area is defined by sofas.

house

mar vista, california
ain, johnson, & day
1946–49
addition by daly genik
1995

On the next block from Dubin and Cheselka, a scholarly couple who moved here in 1980 were faced with a similar challenge of cleaning, stripping, and upgrading—but were less fortunate in their choice of contractor. He is a librarian at the Getty Research Institute, she is a professor of Slavic studies at UCLA, and their top priority was a place to display books and vintage textiles. To create a lofty new space to the rear of the house, they selected the local firm of Daly Genik, whose pared-down, unpretentious buildings evoke Ain's spirit.

"There's a covenant in Mar Vista that bars second stories, but we were able to go up to eighteen feet because the addition is largely concealed from street and doesn't look down on anyone's garden," says the librarian. Kevin Daly devised a lofty space of steel-braced concrete block walls, cut away at two corners to accommodate sliding glass windows. A double layer of translucent polycarbonate sheeting forms a valance attached to slender steel columns that lighten the structure, and contains blinds that are activated by sun. The corners establish a diagonal axis, reinforcing that in the old house, and there is a pleasing dialogue between the vertical mass of the addition and the delicate horizontality of the original. When both corners are open, the cantilevered steel bookshelves on the back wall appear to be a free-standing plane.

Light reflects off a pool onto the maple ply ceiling, with its suspended track lighting, and the polished concrete floor. Two maple boxes flank the opening from the house and contain sliding screens for the display of textiles—picking up on the sliding walls that were an integral part of Ain's design. Hearth and chimney are wrapped with the same wood. To set off the new structure, Daly persuaded the late Garrett Eckbo, who landscaped the Mar Vista development, to send plans for a jewel-like garden.

Above A new library-gallery opens at the corners to a garden designed by Garrett Eckbo

Opposite The eighteen-foot-high addition is concealed from the street and is lightened by a valance of polycarbonate sheeting.

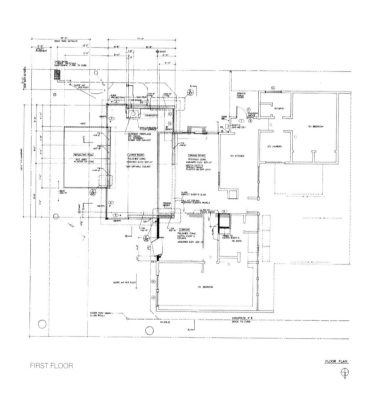

FIRST FLOOR

FLOOR PLAN

Left Light reflects off a pool onto the maple ply ceiling, bathing the interior in a soft glow.

wolf house

weston, connecticut
mies van der rohe
1955–56
additions by peter l. gluck
1981–89

Most architects would be intimidated by the prospect of extending a building by the greatest modern master of form and detail, but Peter Gluck made two successive additions to this 2,100-square-foot villa, creating an extraordinary fusion of old and new. Inspired by an unrealized plan for workers' housing, Mies's steel-framed rectangular box was designed for Morris Greenwald, the brother of Herbert Greenwald, who commissioned the Lake Shore Drive

Apartments in Chicago. Windows left over from the construction of that landmark structure form the side walls of this modest residence, which was conceived soon after the completion of the Farnsworth house, and occupies a similar site. In 1960, Mies substituted double for single glazing on both window walls, and made a seamless addition of two bays.

Twenty years later, a new owner decided to use the house as a weekend retreat, and commissioned Gluck to make additions. "The challenge was to respect this icon of high modernism—by then a historical object—without mimicking the original," the architect observes. "With respect to Mies and history, the design had to be

contextual; with respect to the new owners, it had to function for their needs better than the original could."

Two steel and glass pavilions were set at right angles to the house and tied together with a consistent cornice line, a steel

screen, columns, and paving that extend Mies's grid. One pavilion contains a pair of guest rooms, a sauna, and a Japanese soaking tub; the other, an entertainment area with a small kitchen. The ground plan borrowed from the geometry of

Opposite The paving and metal screen extend Mies's grid, tying together the house and two detached pavilions.

Above In enlarging the original house, Gluck created a dining area to establish a cross axis to the new master bedroom.

Overleaf The challenge was to respect this icon of high modernism without mimicking the original.

FIRST FLOOR

the Barcelona Pavilion. The architect also drew on his experience of working in Japan in the early 1970s, creating raised platform floors and glass walls that slide back into pockets like shoji screens. This gives these two structures the character of open gazebos that complement the formal enclosure of the house.

In 1987, Richard and Jane Wolf, a couple with two children who wanted to live here full-time, asked the architect to design a new master suite. The suite flows out of the original house, creating a bold cross axis that contains a new kitchen and defines a new dining area. Gluck employed horizontal steel windows to distinguish the new construction from the vertical fenestration of the old, and treated the master bathroom as a cubist glass sculpture. The new structures form a complex that extends out into the landscape, shifting constantly as you move around it.

201

Opposite Furniture designed by Le Corbusier enhances Mies's living room

Above The new master bathroom is treated as a cubist glass sculpture.

Top The new master bedroom extends from the rear of the original house.

gross house

rye, new york
ulrich franzen
1956
addition by david earl gross
1997

The modest house that Franzen built for a photographer friend won an American Institute of Architects Honor Award, but it was always an anomaly in this affluent dormitory for Wall Street brokers—by virtue of its size (a mere 1,800 square feet), purity of line, and inexpensive construction. A glass cube shaded by a roof plane cantilevered out from four posts, and flanked by white brick blocks containing tiny bedrooms and a kitchen, it occupied a leafy 1.3-acre site.

This made it an ideal candidate to tear down and replace with a McMansion. It owes its survival to David Gross, an architect in the New York firm of GF 55, who bought it in the wake of the 1987 market crash.

He and his wife Kim, who currently edits the Chic Simple books, had two small daughters and decided they must give up their Tribeca loft. The shift of scale could have been disconcerting, but, as Gross observes, "I learned a lot by living in a house I would not have designed myself." After eight years, he created a two-level, 2,000-square-foot addition that gave the teenagers their own spaces—plus a family room— and that allowed him to upgrade the existing house, installing a

new kitchen in what was formerly a bedroom. Accents of bold color, elegant built-ins, and classic modern furniture enliven the light-filled interior.

There is a lively dialogue between old and new. Symmetry plays off asymmetry, and a glass entry link maintains the rhythm of solid and void. The addition takes advantage of a drop in the grade to reduce the overall height and to engage Franzen's roof plane. Banded brick walls wrap around a latticed grid of

marine-grade plywood, and both are painted white to unify the composition. As Gross notes, this is a contextual work that is abstracted from the original—a product of his training at the University of Pennsylvania. Whereas the old house was a discrete object, detached from its surroundings, the form of the new is generated by its interior spaces—and the entry court, low walls, and indoors-outdoors slate paving weave it into the landscape.

Above A two-story addition creates a lively dialogue with the original house.

Opposite Symmetry plays off asymmetry in this juxtaposition of new and old. (Photo by Durston Saylor, courtesy of *Architectural Digest*)

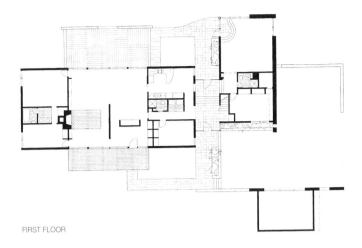

FIRST FLOOR

Opposite A glazed bridge links the two structures. (Photo by Durston Saylor, courtesy of *Architectural Digest*)

Above The new and original houses seem to dance around each other, leading and following.

Left and opposite At the center of the original house, a free-standing screen divides the sitting and dining areas.

harvey house

208

los feliz, california

john lautner

1950

restored 1998 – 99

John Lautner apprenticed to Wright and broke away to become a solitary genius. He scorned convention and enlarged the potential of residential architecture—in southern California and beyond—exactly as Schindler had done two decades before. Both had to struggle for clients who shared their vision; both were underrated in their lifetimes and acclaimed posthumously. However, from the 1960s on, Lautner (though always strapped himself)

benefited from the rise of affluence and was able to build on a heroic scale. Even so, he often had to contend with inadequate materials and technologies, as well as the irresponsibility of later owners.

His first rich client was Leo Harvey, who gave his name to an aluminum company and made a fortune from the invention of the pop-top can. The 5,000-square-foot house he commissioned on a hilltop site in central Los Angeles marked a transition from the intimate, woodsy residences of the 1940s to the long spans and soaring vaults for which he is best known. In the original plan, a wedge of rooms, a rectalinear bedroom wing, and a carport intersect a circular canopy of

glulam beams that extends beyond the entry as a pergola. Wood hoops brace the beams and radiate out like ripples from a central column, which is clad in Arizona stone. Harvey demanded luxurious woods and colored marble, but overwhelmed the architecture with faux medieval tapestries and pompous furniture, enclosed the pergola, and knocked down walls, embittering the architect. A second owner turned the house into a construction site, but never completed what he had begun.

Screenwriter Mitch Glazer and actress Kelly Lynch had already restored a Neutra house at Lone Pine, on the edge of the Sierras, when they saw an advertisement for this house.

They immediately realized its potential. "It was like looking at an aged movie star and thinking how gorgeous she must have been," says Lynch, "only with a house you can perform surgery to restore that beauty." Her husband realized the previous owner had failed to understand what he possessed and had tried to normalize it by pushing out rectangular rooms, but "the house fought him every inch of the way—and won."

It took the couple a year, working with a team of Lautner veterans, including architect Helena Arahuete and veteran contractor John de la Vaux, to complete a major restoration. They removed 2,000 square feet of additions, replaced all the mechanical services, and

Opposite A new rounded copper roof canopy was added during the restoration of a house that had been grossly abused.

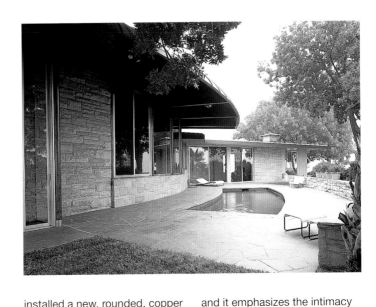

211

installed a new, rounded, copper roof canopy. "We thought we'd do a third of the work and move in, but then we saw how beautiful the finishes were under the grime and water damage," says Glazer. "We all got inspired and spent triple the time and money to get it right." One day they contemplated a massive collar that had been wrapped around the rotunda, blocking the view from the entry, and spontaneously attacked it with hammers. More often, the restoration was a laborious process of removing steel, replacing under-floor pipes, and uncovering the beauty of bleached mahogany paneling and wood block floors.

Glazer and Lynch decided to leave the rotunda enclosed, for Lautner had made the change,

and it emphasizes the intimacy of the rooms that open out of it. Spiky chandeliers gleam off the slate pavers, and the mahogany paneling has been extended and darkened to pull the space together. Like a film spool unwinding, leading your eye to the panoramic view of the Hollywood Hills, the Los Angeles basin, and the ocean, it is a powerful symbol of the house. The couple has decided not to replace missing rings, but to accept the scars as part of the patina of age that makes this 50-year-old house so appealing.

Adolf Loos, the early twentieth-century master of luxurious modernism, would have applauded Lautner's flourishes—including the hearths and rounded chimneys, clad in pink

Opposite Laminated beams radiate from concrete columns to form a rotunda that was originally open to the sky.

Above Boldly grained paduca paneling plays off a cork floor and a rounded work surface in Mitch Glazer's office.

Top A curved pool emphasizes the circularity of the house, which occupies a hilltop that commands a 360-degree view.

213

and green marble, which resemble models of the house. Motorized shutters close off the bar, and a massive vintage television is built into the paneling of the living room. The bathrooms are unabashedly sybaritic, and in Glazer's office, bold grained paduca paneling plays off cork floors and a rounded work surface.

The house is a work in progress, full of difficult judgment calls. The expanded kitchen may be cut back and the original St. Charles cabinets reinstalled. The rotunda will be refined and there is a possibility of recreating the aluminum-framed glass breakfast nook—a kind of high-tech gazebo—originally located under the pergola. Meanwhile the owners and their small daughter adore living here. "At night, we can look all the way through and out at the lights of the city," says Lynch. "I find myself caught up in the spirit of the place, wander about, and forget I'm in the middle of watching a movie!"

Opposite Radial beams impart a lively rhythm to the living room, which opens out of the entry rotunda.

Above The pink and green marble fireplaces resemble models of the house.

Top The master bedroom projects from the body of the house like a cog on a wheel.

goldstein house

beverly hills, california
john lautner
1963
enhanced and extended
1981 –

No second act in recent memory is as astonishing as this: a dramatically sited 4,100-square-foot house of great power and originality that Lautner designed nearly 40 years ago and was invited back to recreate as perfectly as he knew how. It was commissioned by Paul and Helen Sheats, whose enthusiasm for the architect was constrained by their limited means; they stayed only a few years. New owners abused the house, but it quickly found its white knight in James Goldstein, a real estate investor who grew up in Wisconsin and developed a passion for the buildings of Wright. "It was in horrendous condition, but the lines were magnificent," he recalls. "I decided to wait until I could afford to make improvements in the best possible way—though I never dreamed how much I would end up doing."

The house clings to a precipitous slope, looking west to the ocean. A single-story wedge of bedrooms for the Sheats's five children (now remodeled as an office and guest suite) and a kitchen-dining area lead into a living room that begins as a womblike enclosure, then soars within an angular canopy. The owners loved to camp out under the stars, so the architect set 750 water glasses into the waffle-grid concrete vault to admit splashes of sunlight. The interior was left open to the pool terrace, protected only by a curtain of forced air, but this proved impractical and was soon replaced with windows.

Goldstein's first request to Lautner, in 1981, was to replace the house's heavy steel mullions, which cut into the view, and substitute half-inch sheets of tempered glass, butted together. Until then, the owner had been working by himself, sandblasting gaudy paint from the exposed

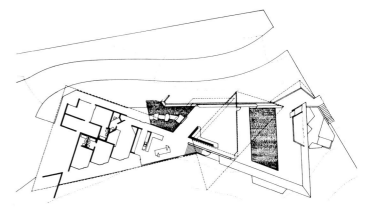

MAIN LEVEL

Opposite An angular concrete canopy over the living room frames the pool and a panorama of Los Angeles.

216

concrete walls and replacing green shag carpet with textured rugs that enhance the concrete aggregate floors. At this point, he began to work closely with Lautner and Helena Arahuete, who took over his office after his death in 1994. "Each step led logically to the next and established a standard to follow," Goldstein explains. "I wanted to remake the house exactly as John would have wanted it, and to introduce technology that didn't exist 30 years ago. It took a long time to achieve perfection, allowing for sketches, models, and mock-ups of each stage.

Plaster ceilings and terrace canopies were recovered in redwood. A wall of rocks around the living room fireplace was stripped away, and a low concrete bookcase was constructed along the south wall. New kitchen cabinets of stainless steel and bubinga wood, topped with polished concrete, replaced Formica. Skylights were enlarged and motorized. A tiny skylit guest bathroom was enlarged to infinity by covering the walls with mirror glass. Plaster walls at the front of the house were rebuilt in concrete, its rough texture playing off the mitered glass and oiled wood. Lautner installed concrete tables and leather-cushioned seating in the living room and den to complement the built-in glass and concrete dining table. The most dazzling transformation had come earlier in the master suite, which is tucked into the hillside, looking into the

Above Panels of tempered glass are butted together to form an invisible barrier between the living room and the pool.

Top A skylight with roll-back glass illumines a glass dining table that is supported on concrete piers.

Opposite Sculptural built-ins complement the spatial drama of the living room.

pool through portholes. Unframed walls of glass roll back to either side of the wedge-shaped bedroom, turning the cantilevered floor into a giant open springboard.

Invention and craft are fused in this house—from the geometry of the steel entry gate, to the angular concrete blocks that step across a pool, past walls of glass, to the peaked vault that frames the sky and distant towers. There is a sense of ceremony as the vista unfolds. Look back, and the four natural elements come together: fire from a corner hearth, water splashing from a rocky hillside, a current of air from the ocean wafting through spaces that obliterate the divide between indoors and out. The house

is filled with light, and every few steps bring a fresh perspective.

The sense of discovery continues as one descends into Eric Nagelman's luxuriant hillside garden, with its winding path, tropical plantings, and environmental sculptures. Duncan Nicholson, who also worked with Lautner, will supervise construction of a tennis court and guest pavilion, linked to the house by an enlarged south terrace. Uncompromisingly, modern architecture embraces nature, fulfilling the dreams of the pioneers, and pointing forward to even bolder experiments.

219

Opposite Concrete blocks step across a pool past walls of glass and a waterfall to the main entry.

Above Motorized glass walls roll back, turning the master bedroom into a springboard poised above the lights of Los Angeles.

Top Beyond the triangular couch is the sleeping area and wall ports that look into the swimming pool.

acknowledgments

Researching this book was a joy, thanks to the owners and architects named in these pages, who extended cordial welcomes and freely shared their passion and expertise. Many other dedicated professionals gave me invaluable recommendations and assistance, without which I would have missed some of the most exciting houses featured here (and a few that I had, reluctantly, to omit). They include A.C. Lellis Andrade, Sergio Apodaca, Susan Bandes, Tim Barton, Nancy Bavinger, Michael Deasy, Herbert Beckhard, Sarah-Ann Briggs, J. Carter Brown, Frances Campani, Julia Converse, Jim Dennis, Christopher Domin, John Eifler, Frank Escher, Jeffrey Fink, David Fixler, Alan Goldberg, John Howey, Elaine Sewell Jones, Joseph King, Jeff Koerber, Wendy Kohn, Peter Loughrey, Chandler McCoy, David Macrae, Tony Merchell, Dietrich Neumann, Chad Overway, Elaine Pfeiffer, Pippa Scott, Gregory and Stefanie Ross, David Serrurier, Judith Sheine, Barry Sloane, Elizabeth Smith, Kathryn Smith, Arlene Stern, Diane Viera, Brian Tichenor, Marc Treib, John Vinci, Susan Waggoner, Hope Warschaw, Cliff Watts, David and Nelia Woodruff, and Marianne Zephir.

Special thanks to Richard and Sandra Bergman, who made New Canaan so rewarding, and to the infinitely resourceful Richard Koshalek. Roger Straus's unfailing good humor and patience were a delight, and his photographs have captured the spirit of these houses. For additional photography and drawings, my thanks go to James Ashby, Steven Ehrlich, Roberta Frey Gilboe, David Earl Gross, Weston Havens, Pierre Koenig, Jack Kraigie, and Amy Murphy, as well as to Lise Bornstein and Jeff Whyte for the plans they skillfully redrew. This book owes much to two editors: Richard Olsen, who commissioned it, and Terence Maikels, who shepherded it to completion.

—M.W.

photo credits

All photographs were taken for this book by Roger Straus III, except for:

Tom Bonner (courtesy of Steven Ehrlich): page 156

Courtesy of Henry Ford Museum & Greenfield Village: page 61 (both)

Courtesy of Henry Ford Museum & Greenfield Village and William
Graham Foundation: page 59

Balthazar Korab (courtesy of Cranbrook Academy of Art Museum):
pages 36, 39, 40, 41 (both)

Courtesy of Jack Kraigie: page 27

John Linden (courtesy of Steven Ehrlich): page 159 (top)

Man Ray (courtesy of Weston Havens): page 87

Durston Saylor/© Architectural Digest, Conde Nast Publications, Inc.:
pages 203, 204

Tim Street-Porter: pages 63, 64, 65, 75

Michael Webb: pages 28, 29 (top & bottom), 33 (top), 35 (top & bottom),
38, 44 (bottom), 60, 66 (top & bottom), 68, 69, 73 (top), 85 (left & right),
91, 94, 96 (left), 119 (bottom), 131 (top), 136 (bottom), 137 (top), 143
(top), 149 (top), 153 (bottom), 186 (bottom), 201 (bottom), 202, 213
(bottom)

Previous spread: John Johansen's Villa   **Opposite:** Richard Neutra's Lewin house
Ponte